THE LIVING TRUST MIRACLE

ESCAPE PROBATE, SLASH ESTATE TAXES, AND LEAVE A LASTING LEGACY

Tammi Schneider

CONTENTS

INTRODUCTION

When Sarah's father passed away unexpectedly, she was devastated. As if the emotional toll wasn't enough, she soon found herself navigating a complex web of legal proceedings, endless paperwork, and mounting expenses. Only then did she realize that her father had never created a living trust.

What was the result of not creating a living trust?

A lengthy probate process that drained the estate's resources and left the family in a state of financial limbo for months.

We hear countless stories like Sarah's of adults struggling after minimal or poor estate planning. It's a common misconception that living trusts are only for the wealthy or elderly. In reality, they are powerful tools that can benefit anyone seeking to protect their assets, minimize taxes, and ensure a seamless transfer of wealth to their loved ones.

For my own story and personal experience, when my mother lost her husband, we saw firsthand how much time and expense came from probate. The attorney who originally drafted the will for her and her husband had done little to protect the assets. They both thought it was the best outcome for his estate, and she would benefit from how he'd drafted the will. But after many months and the dwindling estate funds, she learned that this process benefited the courts and the attorney. She was left with nothing.

That's the reason why I wanted to write this book, "The Living Trust Miracle: Escape Probate, Slash Estate Taxes, and Leave a Lasting Legacy." I set my goal to empower the layperson with the knowledge to take control of their future and their estate, offering insights to assist their planning and the journey to creating a lasting legacy. I do this by breaking down the concepts into bite-sized pieces so they are easily understood and assimilated into any estate planning journey.

In these pages, you'll find many advantages to living trusts. You'll discover how the traditional will and subsequent probate are not always the best option(s) we've been taught. Those wills and probate can cost your family time and money, and create stress during a time when they should be able to grieve. You'll learn how a living trust helps keep your legacy whole and safe from potential liability, including creditors, estate taxes, all while keeping everything together that you've worked so hard to create.

You see, this book isn't just going to show you the benefits of a living trust, but will help you understand the myths surrounding them and why it's not just for the rich, elite people, but for you and me; it's also about dispelling the myths and misconceptions about living trusts. I'll talk about common questions like, "Don't I need an attorney to set one up?" and "Why didn't anyone tell me this before?"

By the end of this book, you'll clearly understand what living trusts are, how they work, and whether they're the right choice for your unique situation.

As with most books, each chapter builds upon the previous one, taking you on a journey from the basics to advanced strategies of estate planning so you can maximize the power of your living trust. You'll learn howto choose the right trustee, navigate the funding process, and keep your trust up-to-date as your life and circumstances change.

However, knowledge alone isn't enough; that's why I've included worksheets and a checklist including plenty of real-life examples to help you apply what you've learned. This book is designed to be a hands-on resource,empowering you to take action and create a comprehensive estate plan that reflects your values and goals.

As you embark on this journey, remember that estate planning isn't just about numbers and legal jargon; it's about securing your legacy and providing for the people you love. You're giving your family a gift.

So, whether you're just starting to build your wealth, are part of a growing family looking to protect your assets, or a retiree seeking to leave a lasting legacy, this book is for you. With the right knowledge and tools, you can create an estate and a legacy that will leave you feeling empowered and at peace, knowing you've taken care of your loved ones even once you've gone.

Let's dive in and discover the living trust miracle together.

Understanding the Basics

There was a time when David, a diligent accountant, assumed his meticulously drafted will was all the estate planning he needed. Confident in his preparations, he believed his assets would seamlessly transfer to his children upon his passing. It wasn't until a close friend faced unexpected delays and costs due to probate that he realized the limitations of a will.

David discovered that a living trust could have prevented these challenges, offering greater ease and efficiency. This realization led him to re-evaluate his estate planning strategy, seeking tools that could better protect his family's legacy.

What is a Living Trust?

At its core, a living trust is a legal arrangement created during your lifetime to manage and distribute your assets after death, bypassing the need for probate. This can be a significant advantage because probate, the court-supervised process of validating a will, can be both lengthy and public, not to mention expensive. By setting up a living trust, you maintain control over your assets while you're alive and ensure they pass smoothly to your beneficiaries after you're gone. Unlike a will, which only takes effect after death, a living trust operates during your lifetime, providing flexibility and control while you're around to oversee it.

The purpose of creating a living trust extends beyond just avoiding probate. It offers a flexible mechanism for managing assets, which is particularly useful if you become incapacitated. With a living trust, the successor trustee can step in to distribute the assets according to your wishes without needing to go to court for permission, which can be a relief during difficult times. This level of preparation can make all the difference, ensuring that your wishes are honored without unnecessary legal hurdles.

When setting up a living trust, you, as the grantor, transfer ownership of your assets into the trust. This means that legally, the trust owns your assets, but you maintain control over them as the trustee. You can choose to manage them yourself or appoint someone else to do so. Upon your passing, a successor trustee steps in to manage or distribute the assets according to your wishes stated in the trust document. This setup allows for a seamless transition of assets without the delays and costs associated with probate.

A living trust can be either revocable or irrevocable, each serving different needs.

A *revocable trust* can be altered or canceled at any time during your lifetime, providing you with the flexibility to adjust the trust as circumstances change. This is an attractive option for those who want to maintain control and make changes as needed.

On the other hand, an *irrevocable trust*, once established, cannot be modified. While this may seem restrictive, it offers distinct advantages, such as protecting your assets from creditors and potentially reducing estate taxes by removing the assets from your taxable estate.

One of the most compelling benefits of a living trust is the privacy it affords. Unlike a will, which becomes a public record after probate, a living trust remains private. This means that the details of your assets and who receives them are kept confidential, protecting your family's personal information from the public. Additionally, while a will can be contested in court, a living trust is generally more difficult to challenge, providing another layer of security for your estate plan.

One example is the Martinez family, who decided to establish a living trust. With multiple properties and a growing investment portfolio, they were concerned about the time and expense of probate. By transferring these assets into a living trust, they ensured that when the time will come, their children would receive their inheritance without the hassle of court proceedings. The trust also allowed them to set specific terms for distribution, ensuring their children received support for education and other needs at appropriate times. This strategic planning provided peace of mind, knowing their legacy would be preserved according to their wishes.

Understanding a living trust is the first step in taking control of your estate planning. It offers numerous advantages, from avoiding probate to providing flexibility in asset management and preserving privacy. By exploring this option, you're not just preparing for the inevitable; you're actively shaping your legacy and ensuring your loved ones are cared for in the way you intend.

Living Trust vs. Will: Which is Right for You?

Choosing between a living trust and a will can seem daunting, yet understanding their core differences makes the decision clearer. At first glance, both serve to distribute assets, but their functions diverge significantly. As stated earlier, a will only activates upon your passing, requiring probate—a legal process that validates the will and oversees the distribution of your estate. Probate can be cumbersome, dragging on for months, even years, making it a public affair that exposes your private affairs to scrutiny.

In contrast, a living trust is designed to take effect during your lifetime. It allows you to manage and transfer wealth privately, bypassing the probate process altogether. This feature alone can save your heirs time, money, and stress, as they avoid the complexities and delays inherent in probate.

Flexibility is a key distinction. A living trust, especially a revocable one, offers the advantage of adaptability. You can amend it as your circumstances or intentions change, ensuring your estate plan remains aligned with your evolving life. On the other hand, a will, while simpler to draft, lacks this flexibility once it enters the probate process. Any changes require more formal needs. A **codicil** is a legal document that amends an existing will. It allows a person (the testator) to make modifications, additions, or revocations to their will without having to create an entirely new one. This rigidity makes it less ideal for those with dynamic financial situations or familial structures that might change over time.

Consider the scenario of managing a large or complex estate. Living trusts shine in such cases by simplifying the transfer of diverse assets. If you own out-of-state real estate, a living trust can help streamline the management and transfer of these properties, circumventing the need for separate probate proceedings in each jurisdiction. It centralizes management and reduces administrative burdens.

For smaller estates where the distribution of assets is straightforward, a will provides a legally binding way to ensure that the testator's wishes are honored without unnecessary complications. In cases where probate is not a significant concern—either due to state laws that streamline the process or the absence of contested assets—the simplicity of a will can be highly beneficial.

One of the key advantages of a will is that it clearly defines beneficiaries and specifies how assets should be allocated, making it an effective tool when an estate consists of only a few primary assets. Furthermore, it will play a crucial role in protecting minor children.

Through testamentary trusts, a will enables parents to set aside assets for their children's future and designate trusted guardians to manage these assets until the children reach the age of legal adulthood. This provision is invaluable for parents, ensuring that their children's financial well-being is safeguarded under responsible stewardship.

While a trust may be preferable for those looking to bypass probate, protect privacy, or manage assets over time, a will remains a fundamental and often essential tool for ensuring that an individual's legacy is preserved with clarity and legal authority. With the many benefits of wills, the choice between a will and a trust ultimately depends on the complexity of the estate and the specific needs of the testator and beneficiaries.

Despite their benefits, living trusts often suffer from misconceptions. Many people mistakenly believe trusts are reserved for the wealthy, a notion that deters other individuals from exploring their benefits. Conversely, some perceive wills as outdated or inferior, yet they remain a vital component of estate planning, particularly for their ability to handle guardianship issues and simpler asset arrangements.

In summary, selecting between a living trust and a will depends on your specific needs and circumstances. A living trust might be more suitable if avoiding probate and maintaining privacy are priorities. However, for those with smaller, more straightforward estates, a will offers simplicity and the ability to appoint guardians, which might be all one needs. Understanding these tools allows you to make informed decisions, tailored to your life's unique tapestry.

Dispelling Myths: Who Needs a Living Trust?

In the estate planning landscape, certain myths about living trusts exist, often misleading individuals into thinking these tools are only for the extremely wealthy. The reality is starkly different; living trusts are not exclusive to those with vast fortunes. They offer benefits that extend to a broad range of people. Think of a family owning one or more properties and an investment account. They might assume that a living trust is unnecessary. Yet, this very tool could simply transfer of their assets upon their passing, ensuring their children receive the family's assets. The belief that living trusts are inherently complex and costly may deter many. While setting up a trust can initially seem daunting, the process is often more straightforward than anticipated, especially with the right guidance. Costs can vary, but many find the peace of mind and potential savings in time and hassle well worth the initial investment.

Living trusts cater to a broader audience than one might assume.

Consider a single parent, Alex, who wants to secure his children's future. By setting up a living trust, Alex can appoint a trusted friend or family member as a successor trustee whom can manage the trust's assets for the children until they reach a certain age, ensuring they have access to funds for education and other needs. Most parents with young children can benefit significantly. A living trust enables them to establish specific terms for how and when their children will receive access to the assets, providing a layer of financial security for their upbringing. This ensures that the assets are used responsibly and align with the parents' wishes.

Similarly, imagine a business owner like Maria, who's looking to retire and wants her children to take over the family business. A living trust enables her to outline a clear succession plan, detailing how the business should be managed and who will assume key roles, thereby smoothing the transition and maintaining the business's stability. These examples illustrate the practical applications of living trusts, demonstrating how they address diverse needs and situations. To determine if a living trust is right for you, it's important to evaluate your personal circumstances. Begin by considering your assets and how you would like them managed and distributed. Do you own properties or have investments you'd like to pass down to the next generation? Are there young children or dependents who need financial security and guidance in managing their inheritance? Or perhaps you have a business that you'd like to ensure continues smoothly after you're gone. These factors can significantly influence the decision to establish a living trust.

Personal Estate Planning Needs Checklist:

1. **Asset Complexity**: Do you own property, properties, or investments that you want to pass on seamlessly?

2. **Family Considerations**: Do you have minor children or dependents relying on your financial support?

3. **Business Succession**: Do you have a business that requires a clear plan for future management?

4. **Privacy Concerns**: Is maintaining privacy around your estate important to you?

5. **Avoiding Probate**: Are you looking to bypass the public and potentially lengthy probate process?

By reflecting on these questions, you can clarify whether a living trust aligns with your goals and needs.

The Cost-Benefit Analysis of Creating a Living Trust

When considering a living trust, the first question often revolves around its cost. Establishing a trust involves several financial components, starting with the initial setup. The cost can range from $400 to over $3,000, depending on the complexity, geographic location, and whether you opt for a DIY approach or hire an attorney. Hiring a professional generally provides tailored advice and ensures that your trust complies with state laws and personal wishes, which can justify the higher cost for those with intricate estates. Beyond creation, ongoing maintenance costs should be considered. These may include fees for asset management or trustee services, which can add up, especially if you appoint a professional trustee. However, these expenses must be weighed against the potential savings and benefits a trust can offer.

Probate can consume 3% to 7% of an estate's value, a hefty price that a trust circumvents entirely, making a trust one of the most significant advantages. This immediate cost saving can offset the initial expense of establishing a trust.

As previously stated, a living trust provides peace of mind and privacy, both invaluable yet intangible benefits. It ensures your estate's affairs remain private, unlike a will, which becomes a public record. This can be particularly appealing for individuals who value discretion or have complex family dynamics. The sense of security that comes from knowing your affairs are in order and your loved ones are shielded from unnecessary legal costs, is a significant aspect of estate planning that transcends monetary value.

When comparing living trusts to other estate planning tools, such as wills, it's crucial to consider costs and along with those benefits. A will is generally less expensive to create than a trust, costing around $150 to $600, but this initial saving must be balanced against the potential probate costs. Furthermore, a trust can offer potential tax savings, particularly if structured to take advantage of estate tax exemptions. A will alone does not provide any tax benefits. Thus, while a will may seem cheaper at first glance, the long-term financial implications of probate and potential tax liabilities can make a living trust a more cost-effective solution over time.

To effectively assess whether a living trust is the right choice for you, a structured cost-benefit analysis is invaluable. This involves evaluating both your current financial situation and your long-term estate planning goals. Consider the nature and complexity of your assets, your family's needs, and your priorities. List potential costs, including setup and maintenance fees, and the benefits, such as avoided probate costs and peace of mind. Assign each factor a weight based on its importance to you and calculate the net value of each. This exercise can illustrate the personal benefits that a living trust may offer beyond the general advantages discussed.

By taking this analytical approach, you can make an informed decision tailored to your unique circumstances, ensuring that your estate planning aligns with your financial and personal goals.

Overcoming Legal Jargon: A Glossary for Beginners

Navigating the world of legal jargon can be daunting, especially when it comes to estate planning. However, understanding key terms is crucial in terms of making informed decisions about living trusts. This section serves as a guide to some of the most important concepts you'll encounter. Let's start with the basics. The **grantor** is the person who creates the trust, likely this is you. They decide which assets are placed into the trust and who will ultimately benefit from them. The **trustee** is the individual or institution responsible for managing these assets according to the trust's terms. They ensure that the grantor's wishes are carried out. Finally, the **beneficiary** is the person or entity that receives benefits from the trust, whether it's financial assets, property, or other types of wealth. Understanding these roles is crucial to comprehending how a living trust operates.

A living trust can be either **revocable** or **irrevocable**.

A **revocable trust** enables the grantor to retain control over the trust's assets, allowing for modifications or cancellations as life circumstances change. This flexibility is particularly beneficial for those who anticipate adjustments in their financial or family situation.

In contrast, an **irrevocable trust** cannot be changed without the beneficiary's consent. While this may seem restrictive, it provides key advantages, such as protecting assets from creditors and potentially reducing estate taxes, which we'll discuss later.

Each type serves different needs, and knowing the distinction can help you choose the right trust for your circumstances.

The term **probate** often appears in discussions about estate planning. Probate is a court-supervised process that involves authenticating a will and distributing assets. **Fiduciary duty** refers to the trustee's obligation to act in the best interests of the beneficiaries. This duty ensures that the trustee manages the trust's assets responsibly and ethically. Also, the **testamentary trust** is a trust established through a will and takes effect upon the grantor's death. Unlike living trusts, testamentary trusts are subject to probate, which may influence your choice of estate planning tools.

Understanding these terms isn't just about overcoming jargon; it's about empowerment. A clear grasp of the language used in estate planning enables you to make informed decisions, communicate effectively with legal professionals, and avoid costly misunderstandings.

Approaching legal documents with confidence can seem challenging, but a few strategies can make it manageable. Begin by familiarizing yourself with the key terms and their meanings. This knowledge provides a solid foundation for understanding the more complex language in legal documents. Break down the document into sections and tackle each part individually. Don't hesitate to take notes or highlight areas that need further clarification.

Seeking resources like online glossaries or legal guides can also be invaluable. Many resources are designed for laypeople, providing explanations in clear, straightforward language. Consider consulting with legal professionals if you encounter particularly complex issues or need personalized advice. Take, for example, a couple who misunderstood their trust's terms due to unfamiliarity with the legal lexicon. This oversight led to unintended tax liabilities and family disputes. By learning the vocabulary and applying it to their situation, they could correct the issues and align their trust with their intentions.

By understanding the terms and concepts, you gain confidence and control over your financial future. With this knowledge, you can ensure that your estate plan reflects your wishes and provides for your loved ones as intended.

The Role of a Grantor: Responsibilities and Rights

Being a grantor in a living trust is akin to being the architect of your own financial legacy. You are the person who sets the foundation by creating and funding the trust, deciding which assets to include and who will benefit from them. This role is pivotal because you determine the framework within which your assets will be managed and distributed. The process begins with drafting the trust document, an exercise in foresight where you outline your wishes and appoint a trustee to execute them. Once the trust is established, funding it involves transferring ownership of your chosen assets—be it real estate, stocks, or personal belongings—into the trust's name. This transfer is essential, for the trust will not function as intended without it.

As a grantor, you retain significant rights and powers. You are not just a passive supervisor but an active participant in managing your trust. You hold the reins on asset management. In a **revocable trust**, you can modify or revoke it entirely, ensuring it remains aligned with your changing circumstances. This adaptability allows you to update the trust to reflect life events such as marriage, divorce, or financial changes. The flexibility of a revocable trust is a valuable tool, enabling you to easily respond to unforeseen events and evolving family dynamics. The trustee executes the trust's terms, but your decision-making authority sets the course. You can direct investments, change beneficiaries, or alter distribution schedules, ensuring that the trust aligns with your current objectives.

However, the role of a grantor comes with its set of challenges. The complexity of administering a trust can be daunting. It demands a keen understanding of financial management and legal nuances, which can be overwhelming for those unfamiliar with such responsibilities. Additionally, family dynamics can pose significant hurdles. Disagreements among beneficiaries, especially if expectations differ from the trust's provisions, can lead to conflicts. As the grantor, you might find yourself mediating disputes or defending the trust's terms, which can strain relationships and test your resolve.

To effectively manage these responsibilities, clear documentation and well-structured estate planning are essential. While regular communication with beneficiaries may not always be necessary, ensuring that your trust's terms are clearly outlined can help prevent future misunderstandings. Keeping your estate plan up to date and accessible to your trustee will help ensure a smooth transition when the time comes.

As guarantor, effective trust management also hinges on strategic oversight. Keep meticulous records of the trust's activities, from asset transfers to distribution logs. This documentation not only aids transparency but also provides a clear audit trail, which can be invaluable in resolving disputes. Engaging the services of a knowledgeable attorney or financial advisor can further enhance your ability to manage the trust. These professionals can offer insights into legal obligations, tax implications, and investment strategies, equipping you with the information needed to make informed decisions.

Embracing the role of a grantor is a commitment to safeguarding your legacy and providing for your loved ones. It requires vigilance, adaptability, and a thoughtful approach to planning. Yet, the rewards of a well-managed trust—financial security for your beneficiaries, the fulfillment of your wishes, and the preservation of your family's harmony—are immeasurable. As you fulfill your duties, remember that the trust is not just a legal entity; it is a testament to your dedication to those you care for, a lasting reflection of your values and foresight.

SETTING UP YOUR LIVING TRUST

Imagine standing at the edge of a vast and intricate garden, one that you have the power to shape and cultivate. This garden represents your financial legacy, the wealth and assets you've accumulated through years of hard work. To ensure that it thrives and is passed down to the right hands, you need a clear plan, a blueprint that guides every decision and action. Setting up a living trust is similar to laying the groundwork for this garden, ensuring that every plant and every pathway is intentionally placed to flourish both now and in the future.

This chapter serves as your guide, detailing the steps to transform your vision into a structured reality, allowing you to confidently manage and distribute your assets according to your wishes.

The journey begins with an initial consultation or research phase, a crucial first step in establishing a living trust. This phase involves gathering information, exploring options, and understanding what a living trust entails. Consulting with an estate planning attorney can provide invaluable insights tailored to your unique situation, ensuring that all legal considerations are addressed. Alternatively, conducting thorough personal research can also be beneficial, especially if you prefer a more hands-on approach. The goal during this phase is to build a solid foundation of knowledge, enabling you to make informed decisions as you proceed. Understanding the legal landscape, the types of trusts available, and the potential implications for your estate are all vital components of this foundational step.

Start by creating a checklist for asset documentation, ensuring that all necessary information is gathered and organized efficiently. This checklist should include details of each asset, such as account numbers, property deeds, and any associated paperwork.

Once you have gathered the necessary information, drafting the trust document is the next step. This document is the core of your living trust, outlining your intentions and specifying how your assets will be managed and distributed. Drafting a trust document requires careful consideration and precision, as it must accurately reflect your wishes while adhering to legal requirements. While some may choose to use trust software for this task, leveraging an attorney's expertise can help ensure that the document is comprehensive and legally sound. An attorney can guide you through the nuances of trust language, helping to avoid ambiguities that could lead to disputes or misinterpretations down the line. This step is about putting your plans into writing, creating a clear and enforceable map for your estate.

After drafting the trust document, the focus shifts to funding the trust with assets. Properly transferring ownership of your assets into the trust is essential for it to function as intended. This means retitling assets, such as real estate, bank accounts, and investments, to be owned by the trust rather than you personally. The process can be detailed and requires meticulous attention to detail to ensure that each asset is correctly titled. Failing to fund the trust adequately is a common pitfall that can render it ineffective, as only the assets held in the trust are subject to its terms. Therefore, a thorough asset listing that you have already created serves as both a checklist and a roadmap for this stage. Documenting every asset, you intend to include ensures nothing is overlooked and everything is accounted for. You will find a simple checklist included in this book.

Keeping trust paperwork organized is equally important, as it facilitates easy access and reference. Consider using a dedicated folder or digital storage solution to keep all related documents in one place. This organization not only facilitates the setup process but also streamlines future updates and audits.

Checklist for Asset Documentation:

- **Asset Inventory**: List all intended assets with descriptions and values.
- **Ownership Verification**: Ensure assets are in your name or are readily transferable.
- **Supporting Documents**: Gather deeds, titles, account statements, and relevant paperwork.

- **Trust Titling**: Prepare to retitle assets in the trust's name to ensure compliance.

- **Communication Records**: Document discussions with trustees and involved parties.

This structured approach ensures that your financial legacy is protected, strategically managed, and seamlessly transferred according to your wishes.

Essential Documents: What You Need and Why

When establishing a living trust, understanding the role of each document is crucial. Think of these documents as the building blocks of your trust, each serving a distinct purpose in ensuring your estate plan is legally sound and effective. At the heart of a living trust is the **trust agreement**, a comprehensive legal document that outlines your intentions, details the assets included, and specifies how these assets should be managed and distributed. It is the foundation of your trust, dictating the terms under which your assets will be handled both during your lifetime and after your passing. This document must be crafted precisely to prevent future disputes and ensure your wishes are clearly articulated.

Next is the **certificate of trust**, a streamlined version of the trust agreement that provides proof of the trust's existence. Financial institutions often require this document to verify the trust without disclosing the entire trust agreement, thereby keeping sensitive details confidential. It serves as the trust's "birth certificate," providing a concise overview that includes the trust's name, date of creation, and the identity of the acting trustee. This ensures that entities, such as banks or investment firms, can interact with the trust while maintaining the privacy of its full contents. It simplifies transactions and interactions with third parties, allowing them to recognize and respect the trust's authority without examining the entire agreement.

Another critical element is the property deeds and titles for transfer. These documents facilitate the transfer of real estate and other titled assets into the trust's ownership. Properly executed deeds ensure that properties are legally held by the trust, making them subject to the trust's terms and avoiding probate. Each property must have its deed retitled in the name of the trust, a process that requires careful attention to detail. If your home still carries a mortgage, this is where a legal advisor can help because errors or omissions in this process can lead to significant issues later, potentially rendering the trust ineffective with regard to those assets. Therefore, accuracy is paramount when preparing and filing these documents.

Organizing and preparing these documents requires a methodical approach. Begin with a template for the trust agreement, which can provide a structured format and ensure that all necessary clauses are included. Templates can be acquired from reputable legal resources or through consultation with an attorney who can tailor them to fit your specific needs. Once drafted, consider creating a dedicated folder, either physical or digital, to store all related paperwork. This aids in easy retrieval and updating, a necessity for maintaining an effective estate plan.

The legal implications of document accuracy cannot be overstated. Incorrect or incomplete documentation can lead to disputes, financial losses, and unintended consequences for your heirs. Furthermore, a notary public plays a crucial role in document verification, ensuring that signatures are genuine. Notarization adds a layer of authenticity and can protect against any validity challenges.

By understanding the purpose and importance of each document, you can ensure that your living trust is robust, effective, and aligned with your intentions. This careful preparation secures your financial legacy and provides peace of mind, knowing that your affairs are in order and your loved ones are protected from unnecessary legal complications.

Choosing Between Revocable and Irrevocable Trusts

Understanding the difference between revocable and irrevocable options is vital when it comes to living trusts. A revocable trust offers flexibility by allowing you to modify or completely revoke the trust as your life circumstances change. Imagine it as a flexible financial framework that allows you to maintain control over your assets, adjusting the trust as needed. This flexibility can be invaluable if you foresee changes in your financial situation or family structure.

On the other hand, an **irrevocable trust** is permanent. Once you set it up, making changes becomes challenging without beneficiary consent. This permanence can be a powerful tool for those seeking to protect their assets from creditors or to minimize estate taxes. By removing assets from your personal estate, an irrevocable trust can reduce the taxable estate, potentially saving your heirs a significant amount in taxes upon your passing.

Each trust type has its pros and cons. **Revocable trusts** provide unparalleled control. You can manage your assets and change beneficiaries at your whim. However, this flexibility means the trust offers no protection from creditors during your lifetime and doesn't provide any tax benefits. The IRS treats the assets as part of your estate, subjecting them to estate taxes.

Irrevocable trusts, while rigid, provide asset protection and tax advantages. Once you transfer assets into an irrevocable trust, they are no longer considered part of your estate for tax purposes. This can result in substantial tax savings. Yet, the downside is the loss of control over those assets. You can't easily change the terms or retrieve the assets once placed in the trust. This lack of flexibility can be a drawback, especially if your financial situation changes unexpectedly.

Deciding which type of trust suits your needs involves evaluating your financial goals and family circumstances. Ask yourself: What are your primary objectives? If you want to maintain control and flexibility, a revocable trust might be more appropriate. However, if asset protection and tax minimization are your top priorities, an irrevocable trust could be a better choice. Consider your family dynamics as well. Do you anticipate changes such as marriages, divorces, or the arrival of new heirs? A revocable trust allows for easy adjustments. Conversely, if you have a stable financial landscape and wish to shield assets from potential legal claims, the irrevocable option might serve you better.

Let's explore a couple scenarios to illustrate these choices. Imagine a family with fluctuating income due to varying business fortunes. They might opt for a revocable trust, allowing them to adjust their estate plan as their financial situation evolves. This trust type ensures they can adapt to economic uncertainties, maintaining the ability to modify asset distribution as needed. Now, consider an individual with substantial wealth seeking to protect their assets from creditors while minimizing estate taxes. An irrevocable trust would suit their needs, providing a secure structure that shields assets from legal claims and reduces taxable estate value.

Understanding the characteristics and implications of each trust type empowers you to make informed decisions. Whether you prioritize control or protection, the choice between revocable and irrevocable trusts can significantly impact your estate planning strategy. By carefully evaluating your financial objectives and family circumstances, you can select the trust type that aligns with your goals, ensuring your assets are managed and distributed according to your wishes.

Avoiding Common Mistakes in Trust Creation

Creating a living trust is a powerful strategy for managing your estate, but like any complex process, it's not immune to missteps. One of the most frequent errors is failing to correctly fund the trust. This might involve neglecting to transfer assets into the trust's name, which effectively leaves them outside the trust's protection. Imagine spending time and resources setting up a trust only to discover that your assets are still subject to probate because they were never moved into the trust. This oversight can render your carefully crafted estate plan ineffective, exposing your assets to the very processes you sought to avoid. Failing to properly fund a trust can lead to legal challenges, as the intended protection and benefits of the trust fail to materialize as planned. Beneficiaries may find themselves embroiled in lengthy probate processes, facing financial losses due to unnecessary legal fees and delays.

Another common mistake is failing to update the trust over time. Life changes, such as births, deaths, marriages, or divorces, can significantly impact your estate plan. Yet, many individuals forget to revisit and revise their trust documents to reflect these changes. This can lead to outdated instructions that no longer align with your current wishes or circumstances, potentially causing confusion and disputes among beneficiaries. Additionally, if a trust is not kept current, it may not accurately reflect the grantor's intentions, leading to disputes among heirs. Imagine a scenario where a grantor fails to update their trust after a significant life event, resulting in assets being allocated according to outdated preferences leading to costly legal battles as heirs contest the trust's terms.

The consequences of these errors can be severe. To avoid these pitfalls, adopting a proactive approach to trust maintenance is critical. Regular reviews and updates should be part of your estate planning routine. Set a schedule to revisit your trust documents annually or during a significant life event. Communicate clearly with trustees and beneficiaries about any changes or updates to the trust, if desired. Open lines of communication prevent misunderstandings and ensure that everyone involved is aware of the trust's terms and their roles within it. This transparency fosters cooperation and reduces the likelihood of disputes arising from misinterpretations.

As an example, the Thompson family learned the hard way about the importance of clarity in trust terms. After their father passed away, the siblings discovered that the trust document contained vague language regarding the distribution of certain assets. Disagreements arose over the interpretation of these terms, resulting in an extended legal dispute that strained family relationships and depleted the estate's resources.

Remember, clear, precise language in the trust document could have prevented misunderstandings and preserved the family's unity. By learning from such examples, you can appreciate the value of careful drafting and ongoing management in maintaining an effective trust.

Ensuring that your trust is properly funded and regularly updated is vital. It helps maximize the benefits of your estate plan and provides peace of mind that your assets will be managed and distributed according to your wishes. Avoiding common mistakes involves vigilance, communication, and a commitment to keeping your trust relevant to your evolving life circumstances.

Interactive Workbook: Templates and Checklists

Establishing a living trust might seem like navigating a complex maze, but interactive tools can serve as your trusty guide through the process. Imagine having a map that lays out your route and provides the specific tools needed at each juncture. This is where templates and checklists come into play. A template for drafting trust documents acts as a blueprint, providing a structured format that helps ensure you don't miss any critical elements. It's like having a pre-assembled kit that you can customize to fit your specific needs, allowing you to focus more on the content rather than the structure. A well-designed template can simplify the drafting process, making it less intimidating and more manageable.

Additionally, checklists are your trusty companions, meticulously tracking your progress and ensuring no step is overlooked. A comprehensive checklist serves as a constant reminder of what needs to be done and what's already completed. It breaks down the process into manageable tasks, providing a clear pathway from start to finish. By checking off each task as you complete it, you gain a sense of accomplishment while ensuring that nothing falls through the cracks. This not only keeps you organized but also reduces the chances of oversight.

Effectively integrating these tools into your trust creation workflow requires a thoughtful approach. Start by writing down your wishes of your unique circumstances. This might involve thinking about specific sections to better capture your intentions. Take it step by step, reviewing each section thoroughly and making any necessary adjustments. As for checklists, utilize them as dynamic documents, updating them as you progress. They should evolve with your process, accommodating any changes or additions that arise. Use them as reminders and active participants in your planning, guiding each action and decision.

The value of these resources extends beyond mere facilitation. They transform the abstract concept of trust creation into a tangible and actionable process, empowering you to take control of your estate planning. Errors are minimized because you have a clear, structured approach that leaves little room for mistakes. This ensures a comprehensive trust setup, where every detail is addressed and every asset is accounted for. The result is a robust estate plan that reflects your wishes and protects your legacy.

To illustrate their usefulness, consider a sample trust agreement template. This template provides a framework with sections for identifying the grantor and trustee, detailing asset distribution, and specifying any special instructions or conditions. It serves as a starting point, guiding you through each essential component of the trust. Similarly, a completed asset checklist might include columns for asset description, current ownership, and steps required for transferring ownership to the trust. This checklist ensures you thoroughly document each asset, facilitating a seamless transfer process. These examples highlight how templates and checklists can demystify the trust creation process, transforming it from a daunting task into a manageable, organized endeavor.

Tailoring Your Trust for Unique Family Dynamics

When it comes to estate planning, one size does not fit all. Every family is unique, with its circumstances, values, and goals. This is why customizing a trust to meet specific family needs is so crucial. For families with blended dynamics, for instance, the complexities can be significant. In such cases, it's important to consider how assets will be divided between biological children and stepchildren. A trust can be tailored to ensure that all family members are treated fairly, preserving harmony and preventing disputes. Similarly, if your family holds particular values, such as a commitment to education or philanthropy, your trust can reflect these priorities. You might include provisions for setting aside funds for college tuition or charitable donations, ensuring that your legacy aligns with your beliefs and supports the causes you care about.

Customizing a trust also involves addressing unique family situations. For example, suppose you have a family member with special needs. In that case, your trust can include specific terms to ensure they receive the necessary care and resources without jeopardizing their eligibility for government benefits. This might involve creating a **special needs trust** within your living trust, allowing assets to be used for their benefit while maintaining their access to essential services. Similarly, if your family owns a business, you may want to include provisions for business succession, outlining how the business should be managed and who should assume leadership roles. This foresight can prevent conflicts and ensure the business's continued success, safeguarding both the family's financial stability and its entrepreneurial legacy.

To illustrate the effectiveness of tailored trusts, consider a family spanning multiple generations. They might establish a trust that provides for immediate heirs and sets terms for future generations. This trust could outline conditions for educational funding, home purchases, or starting a business. Doing so ensures that the family's values and resources continue to support the growth and prosperity of each generation. Another scenario might involve a trust managing family-owned properties. The trust could specify maintenance responsibilities, usage rights, and distribution plans for rental income, ensuring equitable and efficient property management. These examples highlight how a well-crafted trust can address diverse needs, preserving both the family's wealth and harmony.

These tailored trusts require communication when it comes to implementing them. Clear and open discussions with family members about the trust's terms are essential to avoid misunderstandings and ensure everyone is on the same page. If desired, regular family meetings can provide a forum for discussing the trust and its provisions. These gatherings provide opportunities for dialogue, enabling family members to express their concerns, ask questions, and gain a deeper understanding of the decision-making process. You can consider whether documenting these meetings is helpful, perhaps with minutes or summaries, so they can serve as a valuable record and reference point. Such transparency fosters trust and cooperation, thereby reducing the likelihood of disputes and enhancing the effectiveness of trust.

In conclusion, tailoring your trust to meet your family's specific needs is more than a strategic move; it reflects your commitment to their future well-being. This chapter has explored how customization can address the unique family dynamics, ranging from blended families to those with special needs and business succession. By crafting a trust that aligns with your values and circumstances, you ensure that your legacy is as unique as your family, providing for their needs today and tomorrow.

Navigating Probate and Tax Implications

When Mark's grandmother passed away, he found himself ensnared in an unexpected web of legal proceedings known as probate. Given her meticulous nature, he had always assumed her affairs were in order. However, the family soon realized that the lack of a living trust meant her estate needed to pass through probate, a process neither swift nor private. As the months dragged on, Mark witnessed firsthand the emotional and financial toll it took on his family. This chapter explores the intricacies of probate, demystifying a process that many find overwhelming and often unnecessarily burdensome.

Probate is a legal process required to settle a deceased person's estate. It involves court-supervised administration to authenticate the deceased's will and oversee the distribution of assets to the rightful heirs. The process begins with filing the will with the probate court, followed by validation of the document to ensure its legitimacy. If the deceased did not leave a will, the court appoints an administrator to manage the estate and distribute assets in accordance with state laws. This process typically involves several steps, including inventorying the deceased's assets, appraising them, and settling any outstanding debts or taxes. The court's role is to ensure that the estate is administered fairly and according to the law, but this supervision comes with significant drawbacks.

Probate has several drawbacks, including time, cost, and privacy concerns. The process can be lengthy, with a median settlement time of thirteen months in some states, and if contested, it can drag on for years. During this time, the estate's assets are tied up and inaccessible to heirs who may urgently need them. Additionally, probate is not an inexpensive affair. It can consume between 3% to 8% of the estate's gross value, with costs arising from court fees, attorney fees, and other administrative expenses. This can significantly reduce the inheritance meant for beneficiaries. The probate process involves public disclosure of the estate's details, including the deceased's financial records, which become accessible to anyone interested. This can be particularly distressing for families, especially those with high-profile estates or those who value their privacy.

For beneficiaries, probate can be an emotionally taxing and financially draining. The delays inherent in probate mean that heirs often have to wait months, or even years, to receive their inheritance, which can be particularly challenging if they depend on those assets. Additionally, the legal fees associated with probate can erode the assets, leaving heirs with less than they expected or needed. This financial impact can be compounded by the emotional toll of navigating a complex legal process while grieving a loved one. The public nature of probate also opens the estate to potential challenges from disgruntled relatives or creditors, further complicating matters and adding to the stress.

Consider this scenario of a family caught in probate delays. After the patriarch's untimely passing, his children found themselves embroiled in a drawn-out probate process. The estate, which included a small family business, was tied up in legal red tape for over a year, during which the business struggled without clear leadership. This delay strained the family's finances and threatened the business's livelihood and that of its employees. Conversely, imagine a high-profile estate where privacy was paramount. In such cases, the public nature of probate can lead to unwanted attention and scrutiny, potentially exposing the family's private matters to public scrutiny or even legal challenges.

Understanding probate and its implications is necessary for effective estate planning. By recognizing the potential pitfalls, you can take proactive steps to mitigate them, ensuring that your heirs receive their inheritance smoothly and without unnecessary legal hurdles. Whether through creating a living trust or exploring other estate planning tools, the goal is to streamline the process, protecting your assets and your family's peace of mind.

Reflection Section: Consider Your Probate Vulnerability

- **Identify Key Assets**: List your primary assets and consider how they would be handled in probate.

- **Evaluate Dependency**: Reflect on whether your heirs might rely on these assets for their immediate financial well-being.
- **Assess Privacy Needs**: Consider your family's privacy concerns and how public probate might impact them.
- **Consider Alternatives**: Explore estate planning options that might bypass or minimize probate's impact, including a living trust.

By taking these steps, you can gain clarity on your current estate planning status and identify areas for improvement.

Living Trusts and Probate Avoidance: Practical Benefits

Living trusts serve as a sophisticated mechanism to bypass probate, offering a more seamless transfer of assets to beneficiaries. At the heart of this process is the direct transfer mechanism, which allows assets to move to the intended recipients without the need for court oversight. This elimination of court involvement is a significant advantage, as it removes the layers of bureaucracy that often accompany probate proceedings. By setting up a living trust, you appoint a successor trustee to manage and distribute the trust's assets according to your wishes. This ensures that your beneficiaries receive their inheritance promptly and without the delays typically associated with the probate court. The trust acts as a private contract, allowing your estate to be handled discreetly and efficiently.

The time and cost savings associated with living trusts are considerable. As we've seen probate can stretch over months or even years, trust administration is generally much quicker. This is because trusts do not require the same level of court supervision, which accelerates the asset distribution process. Financially, the contrast is stark: probate fees can consume a portion of the estate's value, whereas setting up a trust involves a one-time cost that is often significantly lower. This cost-efficiency means more of your estate's value remains intact for your heirs, providing them with a greater share of the wealth you've worked hard to build.

Privacy is another compelling benefit to consider a living trust. This privacy extends to the financial details of your estate, the identity of your beneficiaries, and the specifics of your asset distribution. By avoiding public record filings, a trust protects sensitive information from becoming accessible to the curious public or even potential creditors. This confidentiality is particularly appealing to families who prefer to keep their financial affairs private. With a living trust, your affairs remain known only to those involved.

Another example is the Johnson family who established a living trust to manage their substantial real estate holdings. When the family patriarch passed away, the trust facilitated a quick and orderly transfer of properties to his children. The successor trustee could distribute the assets according to the trust's instructions without delay. In another instance, the Smiths, who valued their privacy, used a trust to manage their estate after witnessing a neighbor's painful probate ordeal. Their trust ensured that asset transfers were handled discreetly, away from public view, safeguarding their personal and financial privacy. These cases illustrate how living trusts can offer both practical and strategic advantages in estate planning.

Understanding Estate Taxes: What You Need to Know

Estate taxes can seem like a daunting labyrinth of rules and numbers, but understanding their impact is imperative for effective estate planning. Essentially, estate taxes are levied on the value of a person's assets at the time of their death. This tax is calculated based on the fair market value of all assets, including real estate, stocks, and personal belongings. At the federal level, the estate tax applies to estates exceeding a certain value, which the IRS sets annually. In 2023, the exemption cap stood at $12.92 million, meaning estates valued below this amount are not subject to federal estate taxes. However, not all states follow federal guidelines. Some impose their estate taxes with lower exemption thresholds, which can catch unprepared heirs off-guard. For instance, states like Oregon and Massachusetts have much lower thresholds, around $1 million, making it essential to consider both federal and state-specific regulations.

The financial implications of estate taxes are significant, directly affecting beneficiaries' inheritance. While the federal exemption is quite high, states with lower thresholds can lead to unexpected tax liabilities. When an estate exceeds the exemption limit, the tax rate can substantially reduce the overall inheritance. This might necessitate liquidating assets to cover the tax bill, which can be particularly painful if it means selling cherished family properties or valuable investments. This financial burden can be unexpected for heirs, especially if they were unaware of the estate's total value or the applicable tax rules. The need to liquidate assets affects the financial landscape and can carry emotional weight, as selling off parts of an estate may feel like losing a piece of family history.

Tax planning becomes indispensable to mitigate these impacts. By employing proactive strategies, you can significantly reduce the estate tax burden. Consider a scenario where an estate planning attorney helps a family utilize gifting strategies to lower their taxable estate. Gifting assets to heirs during the grantor's lifetime decreases the estate's value, potentially placing it below the taxable threshold. This reduces the estate tax liability and allows heirs to benefit from assets sooner.

Gifting during one's lifetime is a tax strategy worth exploring. This involves transferring assets to heirs while still alive, effectively reducing the size of the taxable estate. Gifts can be made up to a certain amount annually without incurring gift taxes, allowing for a gradual transfer of wealth. This approach not only lessens the estate's value at death but also enables heirs to enjoy their inheritance sooner. Consider the case of a grandparent who gifts portions of their estate to grandchildren over several years. This strategy minimizes potential estate taxes and provides financial support to the younger generation when they need it most, such as for education or starting a new family.

Here is where a trust is an effective approach to manage and transfer wealth tax-efficiently. For example, an irrevocable trust can remove assets from the estate, shielding them from estate taxes and ensuring that they are passed directly to beneficiaries without incurring an additional tax burden. These strategies highlight the importance of foresight and planning in estate management.

Understanding estate taxes and planning accordingly can preserve more of your wealth for your loved ones. By staying informed about the tax landscape and employing proactive strategies, you can effectively manage your estate's tax obligations, ensuring that your legacy is preserved for those who matter most.

Tax Advantages of Living Trusts: Saving Strategies

Living trusts offer strategic tax advantages that can optimize your estate's financial outcomes, acting as a shield and protecting against unnecessary financial burdens. One of the primary benefits is the deferral of estate taxes. By placing assets within a living trust, you can effectively postpone tax liabilities until a more favorable time, allowing your estate to grow without immediate tax deductions. This deferral can be particularly advantageous for those with substantial assets, as it provides a buffer against immediate tax implications, offering breathing room to manage and plan distributions effectively.

Moreover, living trusts reduce the taxable estate value. By transferring assets into a trust, you remove them from your personal estate, thereby potentially lowering the overall value subject to estate taxes. This strategic reduction can lead to significant savings, ensuring that more of your wealth is preserved for your beneficiaries. It's a form of financial foresight that aligns with long-term wealth management goals, providing a structured approach to asset protection and tax minimization.

Maximizing tax savings through trusts involves leveraging specific strategies designed to capitalize on these benefits. One such strategy is the use of **charitable remainder trusts**. These trusts not only support philanthropic goals but also offer substantial tax deductions. By donating assets to a charitable trust, you can receive an immediate tax deduction for the gift's present value while retaining an income stream from the trust. At the trust's termination, the remaining assets are passed to the designated charity, ensuring that charitable giving is with tax efficiency.

Another effective strategy is the establishment of **bypass trusts**, often employed to reduce estate taxes. These trusts are crucial for married couples, allowing each spouse to fully utilize their estate tax exemption. When one spouse passes away, the trust holds assets up to the exemption limit, preventing the surviving spouse's estate from exceeding the taxable threshold. This approach effectively doubles the estate tax exemption for the couple, thereby safeguarding a greater portion of their wealth for future generations.

Professional advice plays a vital role in trust-based tax planning, guiding you through the complexities of estate management. Estate planning attorneys and tax professionals possess the expertise to explain legal nuances and tax regulations, ensuring your trust is structured to maximize benefits. They can help tailor strategies to your specific situation, taking into account factors such as asset types, family dynamics, and long-term objectives. Their guidance can be invaluable, minimizing the risk of oversight and optimizing the trust's tax efficiency.

Incorporating these strategies into your estate planning can transform the way you manage and preserve your wealth. Trusts offer a flexible, powerful tool for optimizing tax outcomes, ensuring that your legacy remains intact and your beneficiaries receive the maximum benefit. With professional guidance, you can navigate the complexities of tax regulations and harness the full potential of living trusts to secure your financial future.

Real-Life Scenarios: How Trusts Avoid Probate

For the Adams family, who skillfully navigated estate planning by utilizing a living trust. With a diverse array of assets, including multiple properties and investment portfolios, they faced potential complications upon the matriarch's passing. By establishing a trust, the family ensured these assets were distributed according to the matriarch's wishes, bypassing the lengthy probate process. The trust allowed them to maintain family harmony, as each member received their share without dispute or delay. In another instance, the Carters, a high-net-worth family with substantial business interests, structured their estate plan with innovative trust arrangements. They employed a **pour-over will**, which funneled any remaining assets into an existing trust upon the patriarch's death. This seamless integration ensured that no assets were left unmanaged or subjected to probate. Additionally, they established an **irrevocable life insurance trust**, providing liquidity for estate taxes without burdening their heirs. These strategic choices safeguarded the family's wealth and facilitated a smooth transition of leadership within the family business, preserving its legacy and continuity.

Challenges inevitably arise in estate planning, but trusts offer robust solutions. The Roberts family, for example, faced the daunting task of managing a complex asset structure that included international properties and a family-run business. By utilizing a living trust, they managed these assets more efficiently, consolidating management under a single entity. This approach minimized potential disputes over asset division, as the trust's terms clearly outlined each beneficiary's entitlements. Similarly, if the Thompson family encountered disagreements over inheritance, threatening to escalate into legal battles, trust agreements can incorporate mediation clauses. This successfully resolved conflicts, ensuring a fair distribution in line with the grantor's intentions.

Trusts not only mitigate financial risks but also provide immense emotional relief. The Martins family witnessed a neighbor's probate litigation, so they were motivated to establish a trust to protect their own family from similar turmoil. When the time came, the swift distribution of assets allowed the Martins to focus on healing and remembrance rather than being entangled in legal proceedings. The Smiths, too, benefited from a trust's efficiency; their father had set up a living trust that facilitated an immediate transfer of funds needed for medical expenses. This timely access to resources alleviated financial stress during a critical period, underscoring the trust's role in supporting beneficiaries' immediate needs.

These real-life scenarios showcase the practical advantages of trusts in estate planning. By providing a framework for asset management and minimizing the potential for conflict, trusts offer a pathway to preserving family wealth and harmony. The ability to avoid probate saves time and money, shielding families from public scrutiny and legal entanglements. Through thoughtful planning and innovative trust structures, individuals can ensure that their legacy is protected and their loved ones are supported in the most effective way.

Common Tax Pitfalls and How to Avoid Them

Navigating the world of estate taxes can be like traversing a minefield, with potential pitfalls lurking at every turn. One of the most frequent errors in estate planning is failing to update trust terms in response to changes in tax laws. Tax legislation is not static; it evolves, sometimes significantly, impacting how estates are taxed. Alterations in federal exemption limits or state-specific tax rules can dramatically change your estate's tax liability. If your trust terms are not updated to reflect these changes, you risk exposing your estate to unexpected and potentially substantial tax burdens.

This oversight can result in increased expenses and a reduced inheritance for your beneficiaries, ultimately undermining the very purpose of your careful planning.

A common mistake is overlooking state-specific tax obligations. While federal estate taxes often grab the headlines due to their broad implications, state-level taxes can be equally impactful. Each state has its own set of rules and thresholds, which can vary significantly. Failing to account for these state-specific obligations can result in legal challenges and delays, as your estate may be subject to additional scrutiny or penalties. This can complicate the administration of your estate, leading to increased costs and stress for your heirs. It is crucial to consider where you reside and where your assets are located, as different states may impose varying tax requirements on those assets.

To avoid these pitfalls, regular trust reviews are indispensable. Engaging with tax advisors periodically ensures your estate plan aligns with current laws and regulations. These professionals can provide valuable insights into legislative changes and recommend adjustments to your trust to ensure its ongoing tax efficiency. Incorporating flexibility by allowing for amendments as tax laws change, you create a dynamic plan that can adapt, reducing the risk of negative tax implications. This foresight helps safeguard your estate against unforeseen tax liabilities, preserving its value for your heirs.

Consider the example of a family that faced significant tax challenges due to an outdated trust. When a key tax law changed, their previously untouched estate plan failed to comply with new regulations. The resulting tax burden was substantial, forcing the family to reevaluate their strategy. By consulting with a tax professional, they can restructure the trust to optimize its terms, leveraging current laws and minimizing liabilities. This proactive measure not only resolved their immediate issues but also positioned the estate for future success, demonstrating the importance of vigilance and adaptability in estate planning.

Another case involved restructuring a trust to optimize tax outcomes. The estate was initially set up under assumptions that had since become obsolete due to legal changes. By revisiting the trust with a tax advisor, the family identified opportunities to incorporate tax-saving strategies, such as utilizing charitable remainder trusts and other tax-efficient vehicles. These adjustments enhanced the trust's effectiveness and significantly reduced the estate's tax exposure, allowing more wealth to be passed on to the next generation. Such examples underscore the value of proactive planning in estate management, highlighting how foresight and expert guidance can transform potential pitfalls into opportunities for growth and preservation.

As we wrap up our exploration of probate and tax implications, remember that understanding these complexities is the first step in protecting your estate. By avoiding common mistakes and embracing informed strategies, you can safeguard your legacy and ensure your loved ones are well provided for. Next, we focus on protecting your assets, where we will explore strategies that shield your wealth from creditors and other financial risks.

Protecting Your Assets

Imagine a family heirloom—a delicate porcelain vase passed down through generations. Its value transcends money, embodying stories and memories that bind your family together. Now, envision a scenario where this irreplaceable piece faces the threat of being lost to creditors due to unforeseen financial difficulties. This illustrates the critical need for asset protection, a fundamental aspect of estate planning that safeguards your wealth from various threats. Trusts, particularly irrevocable ones, play a vital role in this protection by creating a legal barrier between your assets and potential creditors. When assets are placed in an irrevocable trust, they are no longer considered part of your estate, thus shielding them from claims by creditors or legal disputes.

Asset protection through trusts offers a robust defense against creditors. By transferring assets into a trust, you effectively remove them from your control, placing them under the management of a trustee. This separation means that creditors cannot easily access these assets, providing a layer of security in the event of financial adversity. For instance, if you face a lawsuit, assets held in an irrevocable trust are typically protected, as they are no longer legally yours. This protection ensures that your wealth is preserved for your intended beneficiaries, free from the reach of external claims.

Trusts also serve as a shield during legal disputes. Consider a scenario in which a business owner faces litigation due to a contractual dispute. Assets within a trust remain protected, as the trust's legal ownership prevents them from being seized to satisfy judgments. This capability makes trusts an invaluable tool for individuals with high-risk professions or those seeking to safeguard family wealth from potential legal liabilities. However, it's important to understand the limitations of asset protection in trusts. Trusts cannot protect against criminal liabilities or fraudulent activities. If assets are transferred into a trust with the intent to defraud creditors, such transfers can be undone by courts, exposing the assets to claims. Moreover, the timeframe for asset protection varies. Assets transferred shortly before a lawsuit or creditor claim may still be vulnerable as courts scrutinize such transfers for potential fraud.

In considering the types of assets typically included in trusts, real estate properties often top the list. These tangible assets benefit from the protection that trusts offer against seizure or forced sale. Investment portfolios, encompassing stocks, bonds, and mutual funds, also find a secure home within trusts, shielding them from market volatility and creditor claims. Personal valuables, such as art collections, jewelry, and family heirlooms, gain a layer of security through trusts, ensuring they remain within the family and are passed down accordingly. Each asset type enjoys specific protections when held in a trust, contributing to a comprehensive estate plan that aligns with your goals.

Reflection Section: Evaluating Your Asset Protection Needs

- **Identify High-Risk Assets**: List assets most vulnerable to creditor claims or legal disputes.
- **Consider Your Professions and Liabilities**: Reflect on your occupation and potential legal risks.
- **Evaluate Family Heirlooms**: Identify personal valuables you wish to preserve for future generations.
- **Assess Current Safeguards**: Review existing asset protection measures and their effectiveness.

Trusts play a strategic role in estate planning for asset protection. Take the example of a family seeking to protect their heirloom collection. By placing these valuables in a trust, they ensure that the heirlooms are safeguarded from potential claims, preserving them for future generations. Similarly, consider an individual with a diverse investment portfolio facing litigation. By transferring their investments into a trust, they shield these assets from legal seizure, maintaining financial stability during tumultuous times. These examples highlight how trusts can strategically enhance asset protection, providing peace of mind and financial security.

Digital Assets: Including Them in Your Trust

In today's digital age, the concept of assets has expanded beyond physical items to include digital assets. These assets encompass everything from online accounts, such as banking and investment portfolios, to cryptocurrencies and NFTs, which are digital representations of value stored on blockchain technology. Your digital presence also encompasses intellectual property such as blogs, digital art, and social media profiles. These digital components are becoming increasingly significant in modern estate planning, as they often hold substantial financial and sentimental value. Yet, despite their importance, many people overlook digital assets when considering their estate plans, potentially leaving them vulnerable to loss or mishandling.

Incorporating digital assets into a trust requires careful planning and documentation. Begin by creating a comprehensive inventory of all your digital holdings. This inventory should include login credentials, security questions, and any relevant instructions for each asset. Consider using a password manager to securely store this information and ensure it is accessible to a trusted individual. Next, appoint a digital asset manager, someone you trust to handle these assets according to your wishes. This person will be responsible for managing, distributing, or closing accounts as specified in your estate plan. It's vital to outline their responsibilities clearly to avoid confusion or mismanagement.

Protecting digital assets also involves navigating various legal considerations. Digital asset laws can vary, and understanding the nuances of compliance is crucial. Some online platforms have specific terms of service agreements that govern how accounts are managed after the account holder's death. These terms can impact your ability to transfer ownership or access to digital assets. For instance, certain social media platforms may not allow account transfers, while others offer memorialization options. To address these complexities, it's advisable to consult with an estate planning attorney familiar with digital asset protection. They can guide you in drafting a will or trust that complies with applicable laws and platform policies, ensuring your digital legacy is preserved.

Let's explore some scenarios to illustrate how digital assets can be managed within a trust. Consider an individual with significant cryptocurrency holdings. By including these assets in a trust, they ensure that their digital wealth is managed and distributed according to their wishes, even if they lack extensive knowledge of blockchain technology. The trust can specify how the cryptocurrency should be accessed and transferred, protecting it from potential losses due to forgotten passwords or market volatility. In another example, imagine a digital artist with a thriving online business. By placing their intellectual property within a trust, they can safeguard their creative works, ensuring that future royalties or sales are directed to their chosen beneficiaries. This approach not only secures the artist's financial legacy but also preserves their artistic contributions for future generations.

Digital assets represent a valuable and often overlooked component of your estate. By taking the time to inventory these holdings, appoint a capable manager, and navigate the legal landscape, you can ensure that your digital legacy is protected. This proactive approach not only secures your wealth but also provides peace of mind, knowing that your digital presence will be handled with care and respect.

Case Studies: Asset Protection in Action

Consider the scenario of Michael, a successful business owner who leveraged a trust for liability protection. Michael's company, thriving in a competitive industry, faced numerous potential legal threats. To mitigate these risks, he established a layered trust structure, which included both domestic and offshore trusts. This strategic setup not only protected his business assets from creditors but also enhanced his financial privacy. By placing his business assets into an irrevocable trust, he effectively distanced them from his personal estate, thereby shielding them from any lawsuits that might arise from his business operations. Furthermore, the offshore elements provided an additional layer of security, safeguarding his wealth from domestic legal battles.

In another real-world example, the Thompson family successfully preserved their wealth across generations using a trust-based strategy. Concerned about the potential erosion of their estate due to legal disputes or market volatility, they opted for a sophisticated trust arrangement. This included the use of **dynasty trusts**, which are designed to last for multiple generations, thus ensuring that their wealth would continue to benefit their descendants without being diluted by taxes or legal claims. The trust protects against short-term market volatility by safeguarding the assets from creditors during market downturns. The trust's terms were carefully crafted to allow for discretionary distributions, giving the trustees the flexibility to allocate funds as needed while maintaining the overall capital. This approach not only protected the family's assets but also provided financial security for future generations, allowing them to pursue education, entrepreneurship, and other opportunities.

The effectiveness of these strategies is evident in the outcomes and benefits realized by both Michael and the Thompson family. For Michael, establishing a trust provided a robust defense against potential lawsuits. Even when his company faced legal challenges, the trust ensured that his personal assets remained untouched, preserving his financial stability and peace of mind. This asset protection strategy allowed him to focus on growing his business without the constant worry of personal financial ruin. The Thompson family, on the other hand, achieved a seamless transfer of wealth across generations. The dynasty trust not only safeguarded their assets from taxes and legal claims but also reinforced the family's legacy by providing a continuous source of support for their descendants. This strategic planning ensured that the family's values and financial principles were upheld, creating a lasting impact.

Analyzing these case studies reveals key takeaways for anyone considering asset protection through trusts. Proactive trust management is imperative; regularly reviewing and updating trust terms ensures that they remain aligned with current legal standards and the family's evolving needs. Engaging expert legal and financial advice is invaluable, as professionals can offer valuable insights into the most effective strategies and structures tailored to your unique situation. They can help tailor trust arrangements to meet specific goals, whether it's liability protection, wealth preservation, or legacy building. Additionally, the use of layered trust structures, as demonstrated by Michael, highlights the importance of diversification in asset protection, creating a comprehensive shield against various threats.

Ultimately, these examples underscore the importance of thoughtful planning and expert guidance in asset protection. Whether you're a business owner facing potential legal challenges or a family aiming to preserve wealth for future generations, trusts offer a powerful tool to achieve these goals. By understanding the strategies employed in these case studies and applying the lessons learned, you can effectively safeguard your assets, ensuring financial security and peace of mind for yourself and your loved ones.

Strategies for Safeguarding Wealth from Creditors

Imagine you've spent years building a secure financial future, only to face unforeseen events that could threaten your assets. Protecting your wealth from creditors is a crucial aspect of estate planning; several strategies are available to consider. Irrevocable trusts stand out as a robust option. By transferring assets into an irrevocable trust, you effectively remove them from your control, creating a legal shield that creditors cannot easily penetrate. Once assets are in the trust, they belong to the trust, not to you personally. This means creditors cannot claim them, offering peace of mind that your wealth is preserved. However, the effectiveness of this protection can vary based on state laws, as some jurisdictions offer more robust defenses than others. Consulting with an estate planning attorney familiar with local regulations is advisable to ensure your strategy aligns with legal requirements.

Another tactic involves leveraging homestead exemptions and asset titling. Many states offer homestead exemptions, which protect a portion of your home's value from creditors. By understanding and utilizing these exemptions, you can safeguard a significant asset—the family home—from being seized to satisfy debts. Additionally, proper asset titling can enhance protection. For instance, holding properties as tenants in their entirety, where applicable, can protect the property from creditors of one spouse, as both spouses own the property together as a single legal entity. This approach adds a layer of defense by ensuring that the asset cannot be claimed unless both parties are liable for the debt.

Trusts further function as barriers through carefully crafted terms. By limiting beneficiary access, you can control how and when assets are distributed, reducing the risk of mismanagement or premature depletion. Discretionary trust distributions play a key role here, enabling trustees to decide when and how much to distribute based on the beneficiaries' needs. This flexibility not only protects assets from creditors but also ensures they are used judiciously, aligning with the trust's long-term objectives. This strategy is particularly useful in situations where beneficiaries might face financial instability or legal issues, as it prevents creditors from accessing trust distributions directly.

While these strategies are effective, they must be approached with caution due to legal limitations and ethical considerations. Fraudulent conveyance laws are designed to prevent individuals from transferring assets to avoid creditor claims. If a court determines that an asset transfer was made with the intent to defraud creditors, it can reverse the transfer, exposing the assets to claims. Therefore, any asset protection plan should be implemented well in advance of any potential legal issues arising. Ethical considerations also come into play, as shielding assets from legitimate creditors may raise moral questions. Balancing asset protection with ethical obligations is essential to avoid reputational damage and legal complications.

Consider a scenario where an individual establishes an asset-protection trust to safeguard their wealth. By placing valuable assets in the trust, they create a buffer that protects against potential lawsuits. This setup not only shields their wealth but also provides a sense of security, knowing that their financial legacy is secure. In another example, a business owner facing legal challenges utilizes a business trust to limit personal liability. By transferring business assets into the trust, they separate personal and business finances, ensuring that personal assets remain protected even if the business encounters financial difficulties. These strategies illustrate how trusts can be tailored to meet specific needs, providing a versatile solution for asset protection.

Expert Tips on Asset Protection for Families

When it comes to safeguarding family wealth, expert advice can be invaluable. Estate planning professionals offer a wealth of insights to help families maximize asset protection. One key piece of advice from estate planning attorneys is the importance of using multiple layers of protection. This might involve combining different types of trusts with other legal structures to create a comprehensive defense against potential threats. Financial advisors often recommend diversifying assets within a trust as a way to spread risk and enhance security. By not putting all your eggs in one basket, you can protect against market fluctuations and economic downturns, ensuring that your family's wealth remains intact even in challenging times.

Regular trust reviews and updates are crucial for effective asset protection. Life is dynamic, and your estate plan should reflect that. An annual review of your trust can help identify any changes that need to be made, whether due to life events such as births or marriages, or shifts in financial circumstances. Updating trust terms ensures that your estate plan remains aligned with your current needs and goals. This ongoing management is not just about making changes but also about reaffirming that your existing strategy still serves your best interests. By maintaining an up-to-date trust, you can avoid potential legal issues and ensure that your intentions are clearly articulated and legally binding.

Engaging legal and financial professionals is a cornerstone of effective asset protection. These experts possess a profound understanding of the legal landscape and financial strategies that can significantly enhance your estate plan. Consulting with an estate planning attorney allows you to navigate complex asset structures with confidence, ensuring compliance with all relevant laws and regulations. A financial advisor can provide insights into wealth management and investment strategies that align with your risk tolerance and long-term objectives. Together, these professionals form a team that supports your asset protection efforts, offering guidance and expertise that you might not have access to otherwise.

For families looking to enhance their asset protection, several actionable steps can be taken. One effective strategy is diversifying trust assets, which not only mitigates risk but also provides flexibility in how funds can be used or accessed. Another approach is to establish family governance structures, such as a family council, to oversee the management and distribution of family assets. This ensures that decisions are made collaboratively and transparently, reducing the likelihood of disputes and fostering a sense of shared responsibility. By implementing these strategies, families can create a robust framework for protecting their wealth, ensuring that their legacy is preserved for future generations.

Addressing Blended Family Dynamics in Trusts

In the intricate tapestry of family life, blended families present unique challenges in estate planning. When you bring together children from previous marriages or relationships, differing expectations often arise. Each family member may have distinct ideas about their share of inheritance, leading to potential conflicts if expectations aren't managed carefully. Imagine a family where a new spouse and children from a previous marriage coexist. The spouse might assume they will inherit a significant portion of the estate, while the children expect an equal division among all siblings. If these assumptions aren't addressed, it can lead to disputes that fracture family bonds.

One effective strategy to accommodate these diverse needs is to establish separate trusts for different branches of the family. This approach enables you to clearly delineate which assets are allocated to which family members, thereby reducing ambiguity and potential disagreements. For instance, you might set up one trust for children from your first marriage and another for your current spouse and their children. This separation ensures that each group receives what you intend, fostering a sense of fairness and clarity. Additionally, you can include specific provisions for stepchildren and biological children, tailoring the trust to reflect the unique dynamics of your family. Such provisions might include terms that address educational expenses for all children or specific bequests that honor previous commitments or promises.

The emotional and legal complexities of blended families can be daunting, but they are not insurmountable. Consider a scenario in which a trust is established to balance the interests of multiple spouses. In this case, the trust might provide for the current spouse's living expenses while also setting aside assets for children from a previous marriage. This structure requires careful planning to ensure that the needs of all parties are met without compromising the overall integrity of the estate plan. Another example might involve incorporating new family members into an existing trust. As family dynamics evolve, updating the trust to include provisions for new additions can prevent future conflicts and ensure everyone is treated equitably.

Effective communication is key in navigating the complexities of blended families. Regular family meetings offer an opportunity for open dialogue, enabling each member to express their expectations and concerns. These discussions can help clarify intentions and align family members on the objectives of the estate plan. When conversations become challenging, the use of mediators can facilitate productive dialogue. A neutral third party can help resolve conflicts, ensuring that all voices are heard and that decisions are made in a collaborative manner. This approach not only fosters understanding but also strengthens family bonds by promoting transparency and trust.

Blended families, with their diverse dynamics, require thoughtful estate planning to ensure harmony and fairness. By recognizing the unique challenges, they present and implementing strategies such as separate trusts and tailored provisions, you can create an estate plan that respects each member's needs. Open communication and the occasional use of mediation can further enhance understanding, reducing the potential for conflict and fostering a cohesive family environment. As we conclude this chapter, consider how these insights can be applied to your situation, ensuring that your estate plan reflects the complexities and values of your family.

Selecting and Working with a Trustee

Imagine you are orchestrating a grand symphony. Each instrument must play its part flawlessly to ensure the music resonates with harmony and precision. Similarly, selecting a trustee for your living trust is akin to choosing a conductor for this complex arrangement of your financial legacy. The trustee is responsible for managing and distributing your assets according to your wishes, ensuring that your estate plan unfolds smoothly without conflict. This role demands a blend of personal integrity, financial savvy, and unwavering commitment, qualities that are essential for effective trust management.

A good trustee embodies integrity and honesty. They are the stewards of your wealth and must act with the highest ethical standards, placing the interests of the beneficiaries above their own. Integrity ensures that the trustee manages the trust transparently, fostering trust and confidence among the beneficiaries. Honesty is equally vital, as it guarantees that all transactions and communications are truthful and forthright, preventing misunderstandings and potential disputes. These qualities are the bedrock of a trustee's role, ensuring that they act as faithful guardians of your estate.

Financial acumen is another critical characteristic of an effective trustee. Managing a trust requires a sound understanding of investments, tax implications, and fiduciary obligations. A trustee with strong financial skills can make informed decisions that maximize the trust's value and ensure its longevity. They must navigate complex financial landscapes, striking a balance between risk and reward to achieve the best outcomes for their beneficiaries. This expertise is crucial, as it enables the trustee to steward the estate's assets wisely, preserving and growing your legacy for future generations.

Impartiality and fairness are essential traits for a trustee, especially when a trust has multiple beneficiaries. The trustee must treat all beneficiaries equitably, taking into account their diverse needs and interests. Impartiality ensures that no beneficiary is favored over another, maintaining harmony and preventing familial discord. Fairness involves making decisions that reflect the grantor's intentions while balancing the rights and expectations of the beneficiaries. A trustee with these qualities can navigate complex family dynamics, ensuring that the trust's administration remains unbiased and just.

Reliability and commitment are paramount for trustees, as their role often spans many years. Trustees must be available to manage the trust's affairs consistently, responding promptly to inquiries and fulfilling their duties diligently. This availability is crucial, as it ensures that the trust's operations are smooth and uninterrupted.

A long-term commitment is also important, as it assures beneficiaries that the trustee will remain dedicated to managing the trust over time. This dedication fosters stability and confidence, knowing that the trustee is fully invested in safeguarding the estate.

Interpersonal skills play a significant role in a trustee's effectiveness. Clear communication with beneficiaries is vital, as it ensures that they understand the trust's terms and their entitlements. This transparency fosters trust and prevents misunderstandings that could lead to disputes. A trustee must also possess the ability to mediate family disagreements, using tact and diplomacy to resolve conflicts and maintain familial harmony. These skills are invaluable, as they enable the trustee to manage relationships sensitively, balancing the needs and expectations of all parties involved.

Consider the example of a professional fiduciary with a strong financial background. This individual combines technical expertise with personal attributes such as integrity and fairness, making them an ideal trustee. Their financial acumen allows them to manage the trust's assets effectively, while their impartiality ensures equitable treatment of all beneficiaries. Alternatively, a trusted family member with strong organizational skills might also serve as an excellent trustee. Their understanding of family dynamics and commitment to the grantor's wishes can provide a personal touch, ensuring that the trust is administered with care and sensitivity.

Choosing the right trustee is a critical decision in estate planning, as the role involves substantial responsibilities and can last for generations. It's important to evaluate potential trustees based on their personal attributes, technical skills, and administrative capabilities. A combination of a professional trustee and a family member or friend as co-trustees is often ideal, balancing skills and personal insights. This collaborative approach ensures that the trust is managed effectively, preserving your legacy and providing for your loved ones.

Trustee Responsibilities: A Comprehensive Guide

When stepping into the role of a trustee, the responsibilities you undertake are both significant and multifaceted, serving as the backbone of effective trust management. At the heart of these duties lies the administration of the trust according to its terms. This involves meticulous adherence to the directives outlined in the trust document, ensuring that the assets are managed and distributed exactly as intended by the grantor. As a trustee, you act as a steward of the grantor's wishes, which requires a deep understanding of the trust's provisions and a commitment to executing them faithfully. This fiduciary role demands not only the execution of duties but also the foresight to anticipate and address potential challenges that may arise.

Managing and investing trust assets is another core duty that falls within your purview as a trustee. This task requires a strategic approach to asset management, striking a balance between the need for growth and the preservation of capital. Your decisions here can significantly impact the trust's overall value, making it essential to employ sound investment strategies that align with the trust's objectives and the beneficiaries' needs. Whether the trust includes a diversified portfolio of stocks, bonds, or real estate, your ability to navigate financial markets and make informed investment choices is crucial. This aspect of your role not only safeguards the trust's assets but also ensures their potential growth for future beneficiaries.

The fiduciary duty owed by trustees encompasses legal and ethical obligations that are foundational to trust management. At the forefront is the duty of loyalty to beneficiaries, which mandates that you prioritize their interests above all else. This requires transparency in actions and decisions, fostering trust and assurance among beneficiaries. Additionally, the duty of care in asset management obligates you to act prudently, making decisions that reflect a careful consideration of all relevant factors. This duty underscores the importance of vigilance and due diligence, ensuring that every action taken benefits the trust and its intended recipients.

The administrative tasks involved in trust management highlight the practical side of a trustee's responsibilities. Record-keeping and reporting are critical, as they provide a clear and accurate account of all transactions and decisions made on behalf of the trust. This documentation ensures accountability and transparency, serving as a reference for both the trustee and the beneficiaries. Tax filings and compliance also fall under your administrative duties, requiring meticulous attention to detail to ensure that all necessary tax obligations are met. Properly managing these tasks not only maintains the trust's legal standing but also avoids potential penalties or legal challenges.

Trustees often face challenges that test their problem-solving skills and adaptability. Managing a complex financial portfolio, for instance, can present difficulties, especially when market conditions fluctuate. In such scenarios, the trustee must remain informed and proactive, adjusting strategies to safeguard the trust's assets. Conflicts among beneficiaries over distributions are another common issue. Here, effective communication and conflict resolution skills become invaluable. By facilitating open dialogue and mediating disputes, you can resolve tensions and ensure that the trust operates smoothly. These scenarios illustrate the dynamic nature of trust management, emphasizing the importance of a trustee to be both adaptable and resilient in the face of challenges.

Reflection Section: Navigating Trustee Challenges

- **Scenario Analysis**: Reflect on potential financial portfolio challenges and outline strategies for proactive management.
- **Conflict Resolution**: Consider approaches to facilitate open communication and mediate potential disputes among beneficiaries.
- **Documentation Practices**: Evaluate your current record-keeping methods and identify areas for improvement to ensure transparency and accountability.

By engaging with these tasks and challenges, you not only fulfill your obligations as a trustee but also play a pivotal role in preserving the trust's integrity and ensuring its success.

Questions to Ask When Choosing a Trustee

Selecting the right trustee is a pivotal task, one that requires careful consideration and thorough vetting. As you embark on this decision, it's crucial to arm yourself with the right questions to evaluate potential candidates effectively. Start by probing their experience with financial management. A trustee's ability to navigate the complexities of financial stewardship is crucial. Ask them about their experience with managing similar asset portfolios or their understanding of investment strategies that align with your estate's goals. This inquiry not only gauges their technical acumen but also provides insight into how they might handle the trust's financial responsibilities.

Conflicts of interest can significantly compromise the impartiality necessary in trust administration. It's essential to understand how a potential trustee would handle such situations. Pose questions about their approach to managing conflicts and their strategies for ensuring that all decisions prioritize the beneficiaries' best interests. Their response will reveal their commitment to fairness and transparency—qualities that are non-negotiable in a trustee. This conversation also provides an opportunity to discuss any personal connections they might have with beneficiaries, ensuring that their judgment remains unbiased and focused on fulfilling the trust's objectives.

Understanding a trustee's values and how they align with your personal and family values is another key component of the selection process. Delve into discussions about their guiding principles and how these align with the purpose of your trust. For instance, if your trust is geared towards philanthropic efforts or preserving a family business, ensure that the trustee shares these values and can make decisions that reflect them. Furthermore, assess their comfort with making difficult decisions, such as resolving disputes among beneficiaries or reallocating trust assets. Their ability to navigate complex emotional and financial landscapes without compromising the trust's integrity is paramount.

Assessing a trustee's ability to handle complex scenarios requires a focus on adaptability and problem-solving. Consider asking whether they have managed unforeseen financial challenges in previous roles. Their anecdotes can provide a glimpse into their resilience and strategic thinking. Moreover, inquire about their familiarity with similar trust structures, as this experience can be invaluable when addressing unique or intricate estate plans. A trustee who demonstrates a history of successfully managing comparable situations is likely to possess the skills necessary to handle the complexities of your trust.

Effective interview techniques are instrumental in evaluating potential trustees. Scenario-based interviews are particularly useful, as they allow you to present hypothetical situations and observe how candidates would respond. These scenarios should reflect both typical and extraordinary challenges that might arise within the trust's administration. Additionally, reference checks serve as a crucial tool for verifying a trustee's reliability and reputation. Speaking with past colleagues or clients can offer an unbiased perspective on their performance and character, providing reassurance that you're making an informed decision.

Selecting a trustee is not merely about ticking boxes; it's about finding someone who resonates with your values, possesses the necessary skills, and can manage the intricacies of your estate with integrity and diligence. Through thoughtful inquiry and careful evaluation, you can ensure that your chosen trustee will effectively safeguard your legacy and fulfill the trust's purpose.

Aligning Trustee Selection with Your Values

Choosing a trustee involves more than assessing financial acumen and administrative skills; it's about aligning with someone who shares your values. This alignment ensures harmonious decision-making, which is crucial in preserving your family legacy and achieving long-term goals. Imagine a trustee who doesn't understand the importance you place on educational opportunities for your grandchildren. Misalignment in such values could lead to discord and decisions that don't reflect your wishes. Therefore, selecting a trustee who understands and respects your values is critical for the trust's success. This ensures that the trust operates smoothly and reflects the principles that matter most to you, maintaining integrity and purpose across generations.

To articulate your values clearly, consider drafting a comprehensive values statement. This document serves as a guide, outlining the principles that should steer the administration of your trust. It could include your commitment to sustainability, a desire to support charitable causes, or the importance of maintaining a family business. Moreover, hosting initial meetings to discuss trust objectives can be invaluable. These meetings provide a platform for open dialogue, where you can convey your expectations and discuss how these values should influence trust decisions. Such discussions set the tone for your relationship with the trustee, ensuring they are aligned with your vision and can administer the trust in a way that honors your legacy.

Evaluating a trustee's understanding of your values involves more than a simple conversation. It requires observing how they respond to hypothetical scenarios that reflect real-life challenges they might face as a trustee. For instance, you might present a situation involving a conflict between immediate financial gain and long-term sustainability goals. Their response can reveal a great deal about their priorities and decision-making process. Establishing regular communication channels is also key. This ongoing dialogue allows for continual reassessment of the trustee's actions and ensures they remain aligned with the trust's objectives. Regular check-ins and updates not only reinforce mutual understanding but also build a relationship of trust and respect.

Consider the example of a trustee who effectively supports philanthropic goals. Suppose a trust is established with the aim of furthering educational opportunities in underprivileged communities. A value-aligned trustee would not only manage the financial aspects of the trust but also actively seek partnerships with educational institutions to maximize impact. Their proactive approach in aligning financial management with the trust's philanthropic intent ensures that the trust's resources are used effectively, fulfilling the grantor's vision. In another scenario, imagine a trustee managing family business interests, ensuring the founder's vision and values guide business operations. This trustee would prioritize decisions that honor the founder's legacy, such as maintaining ethical business practices or supporting local community initiatives. Their commitment to these values not only preserves the business's integrity but also strengthens its reputation and connection to the community.

Aligning trustee selection with your values is not only beneficial; it is necessary for the trust's success. It ensures that the trustee's decisions reflect your intentions and upholds the principles you hold dear. By articulating your values clearly and evaluating a trustee's understanding of them, you can establish a relationship that not only manages your estate effectively but also honors your legacy in every decision made. This alignment creates a trust administration that resonates with your goals, ensuring that your estate remains a testament to your life's work and values.

Trustee Management: Maintaining Oversight

In the complex world of trust management, maintaining oversight of your trustee is crucial to ensure that your estate is being handled with the care and attention it deserves. One effective strategy is to implement regular performance reviews for your trustee. These reviews serve as a touchstone, providing an opportunity to assess the trustee's adherence to the trust's terms and their overall effectiveness in managing assets. By conducting these evaluations consistently, you can identify areas of improvement and address any issues before they escalate. It's a proactive approach that safeguards your intentions and ensures that the trustee remains aligned with the trust's objectives.

Additionally, establishing clear reporting requirements is essential. This involves setting expectations for the frequency and level of detail in the reports that the trustee should provide. Such reports should include updates on asset performance, distributions, and any significant decisions made. This transparency allows you to stay informed about the trust's activities and make adjustments as needed.

Transparency and communication form the backbone of effective trustee management. Regular meetings with the trustee provide a platform for open dialogue, enabling you to discuss the trust's progress and address any challenges that may arise. These meetings can be scheduled quarterly, semi-annually, or as needed, depending on the complexity of the trust. Face-to-face or virtual meetings, supported by technology for real-time updates, ensure that all parties are on the same page. This ongoing communication fosters a collaborative environment where issues can be addressed swiftly and decisions can be made with confidence.

Furthermore, technology can play a pivotal role in enhancing transparency. Through digital platforms, trustees can provide real-time updates on the trust's financial performance, allowing you to monitor activities remotely. This accessibility not only increases transparency but also empowers you to make informed decisions about the trust's management.

Setting performance benchmarks is another key aspect of trustee oversight. Defining key performance indicators (KPIs) helps measure the trustee's success and effectiveness. These KPIs could include metrics such as the trust's asset growth, the timeliness of distributions, and compliance with the trust's terms. By establishing these benchmarks, you create a framework for objectively evaluating the trustee's performance. Periodic trust audits can further enhance this oversight, providing a comprehensive review of financial management and ensuring that the trustee adheres to best practices. Such audits not only assess the trust's financial health but also identify potential risks, allowing you to take corrective action proactively.

Consider a case study where a trustee utilizes quarterly reports to maintain transparency and accountability. In this scenario, the trustee provides detailed updates on the trust's financial status, highlighting any changes in asset value and outlining future strategies. These reports are shared with the grantor and beneficiaries, fostering a sense of trust and collaboration. Another effective practice involves establishing a family council to oversee trust operations. This council comprises family members and trusted advisors who meet regularly to review the trustee's performance and discuss the trust's direction. By involving multiple stakeholders, the family ensures that diverse perspectives are considered, leading to more balanced and informed decision-making.

Example of Family Council Involvement

- **Objective**: To provide oversight and ensure the trust aligns with family goals.
- **Composition**: Includes family members, financial advisors, and legal counsel.
- **Meetings**: Held quarterly to review trustee reports and discuss strategic decisions.
- **Benefits**: Enhances transparency, encourages open communication, and fosters collective decision-making.

These practices illustrate the importance of maintaining oversight in trust management. By implementing regular reviews, establishing clear reporting requirements, and fostering open communication, you create a robust framework for trustee accountability. This approach not only secures your estate's integrity but also ensures that your legacy is preserved for future generations.

Transitioning Trustees: When and How

Sometimes, despite meticulous planning, the need arises to transition trustees. Several circumstances can drive this change. For instance, a trustee might choose to retire or become incapacitated, leaving them unable to fulfill their duties. In these cases, it becomes essential to have a plan in place to ensure the trust's seamless operation. Another scenario might involve a breach of fiduciary duties, where the trustee fails to act in the best interests of the beneficiaries. Breaches can range from mismanagement of funds to conflicts of interest that compromise the trust's integrity. Addressing such issues promptly is crucial for protecting the estate and maintaining the trust of beneficiaries. Recognizing these situations early can help you prepare for and execute a smooth transition, thereby safeguarding the continuity of your estate.

Transitioning trustees involves a series of steps designed to ensure the process is handled legally and efficiently. Initially, understanding the legal requirements for removing a trustee is vital. This could involve consulting the trust document, which often outlines specific procedures for removing a trustee. Legal advice may also be necessary to navigate state-specific regulations. Once the decision to change trustees is made, the focus shifts to selecting and onboarding a new trustee. This requires identifying a candidate who aligns with the trust's values and possesses the necessary skills to manage it effectively. Onboarding should include a thorough handover process, ensuring the new trustee is fully briefed on the trust's details, current operations, and any ongoing issues.

Achieving a smooth transition is paramount to maintaining the trust's stability and ensuring minimal disruption to its operations. Detailed documentation of the transition process is essential. This includes records of all communications, decisions made, and actions taken during the transition. Such documentation provides clarity and transparency, offering a clear reference for all parties involved. Setting clear expectations for the new trustee is another critical strategy. This involves outlining their responsibilities, performance benchmarks, and any specific goals they need to achieve. By establishing these expectations from the outset, the new trustee can step into their role with confidence, equipped to manage the trust effectively from day one.

Consider the example of a planned trustee transition due to retirement. In this scenario, the outgoing trustee might provide ample notice, allowing sufficient time to select and prepare their successor. The transition process would include meetings between the old and new trustees, facilitating knowledge transfer, and ensuring continuity. Alternatively, imagine an emergency trustee replacement necessitated by unforeseen circumstances. Here, the transition might need to happen quickly, with the new trustee stepping in to manage urgent matters immediately. This situation highlights the importance of having a succession plan in place, allowing for swift action in the event of unexpected events.

Successfully managing a trustee transition ensures that the trust continues to operate smoothly, preserving its integrity and fulfilling its purpose. Whether the transition is planned or sudden, careful preparation and clear communication are key to minimizing disruption and maintaining the trust's stability. By understanding the potential reasons for a trustee change and executing the transition process effectively, you can safeguard your estate and ensure that your legacy is preserved for future generations. With these strategies in place, the trust remains a robust and reliable vehicle for managing your estate, even in the face of change. As we wrap up the chapter on trustees, remember that selecting and managing a trustee is as critical as the trust itself. Next, we will explore maintaining and updating your trust, ensuring that it remains aligned with your goals and responsive to life's changes.

MAINTAINING AND UPDATING YOUR TRUST

Picture this: You've spent years crafting a detailed living trust, carefully selecting beneficiaries, and outlining your wishes. It's like setting the perfect table for a feast, ensuring everything is in its place. However, over time, the guest list changes, and new faces emerge while others fade away. Just like a dinner party that requires adjustments as circumstances shift, your living trust needs regular updating to remain effective and relevant. Life is ever-changing, with new milestones and challenges that can alter your financial landscape and personal priorities. Without periodic updates, your trust might no longer align with your current intentions, potentially leading to unintended consequences.

Trusts need regular updates due to the dynamic nature of personal circumstances and legal environments. Families evolve, children are born or adopted, marriages occur, and divorces happen. Each of these events can significantly impact your estate plan. For instance, the birth of a child might necessitate adding them as a beneficiary, ensuring they are provided for in the future.

Similarly, a divorce could mean removing an ex-spouse from the trust, reflecting your new reality. It's crucial to revisit your trust whenever such changes occur, ensuring it accurately represents your current family structure and wishes. Financial status can also fluctuate, with shifts in income or assets requiring adjustments to how your wealth is managed and distributed.

Perhaps you've acquired new properties or investments that need to be included in the trust, or maybe you've faced financial setbacks that necessitate revising your estate plan. Neglecting to update your trust can lead to significant risks and complications. Outdated beneficiary designations are a common issue, potentially resulting in assets being distributed contrary to your current desires.

Imagine the distress of having your estate passed to someone you no longer wish to benefit simply because the trust was not updated. Moreover, failing to align your trust with current tax laws can lead to unexpected tax liabilities, diminishing the value of your estate.

As tax regulations evolve, it's vital to ensure your trust reflects these changes, maximizing tax efficiency and protecting your legacy. Without regular updates, your trust may become misaligned with legal requirements, potentially leading to disputes among beneficiaries and costly legal battles.

To maintain the strength and relevance of your trust, a recommended schedule for reviews is essential. Conducting annual reviews allows you to assess your trust's alignment with your current circumstances and make necessary adjustments. During these reviews, evaluate any changes in your family structure, financial status, and legal environment, ensuring your trust remains comprehensive and effective. Additionally, major life events should trigger immediate trust assessments. Events such as marriage, divorce, the birth or adoption of a child, or the death of a beneficiary or trustee are pivotal moments that warrant updates to your trust. By adhering to a proactive review schedule, you can ensure your trust remains a true reflection of your intentions and priorities.

Consider the scenario of a trust failing to accommodate new family members. Suppose an individual marries and gains stepchildren but neglects to update their trust. Upon their passing, the stepchildren could be inadvertently excluded from inheritance, leading to family discord and potential legal disputes. In another example, failing to address changes in tax laws could result in substantial tax penalties. Imagine a trust that was established years ago, before significant tax reforms.

Without updates, the trust might miss out on available exemptions or deductions, unnecessarily increasing the estate's tax burden. These examples underscore the importance of timely and regular trust updates, ensuring your wishes are honored and your assets are protected.

Call to Action: Schedule Your Trust Review

- **Annual Review:** Set a date each year to assess your trust's alignment with your current circumstances.

- **Life Event Trigger:** Use major life changes as prompts for immediate trust evaluation and updates.
- **Professional Consultation:** Engage with an estate planning attorney to ensure your trust reflects current legal and tax environments.

By keeping your trust up-to-date, you safeguard your legacy, ensuring your estate plan continues to serve your best interests and those of your loved ones.

State-Specific Laws and Their Impacts

Imagine setting up a living trust in one state, only to find out that its provisions are misaligned with the laws of another state you move to.

This scenario underscores the importance of understanding state-specific trust laws, which vary widely and can significantly impact trust administration. Each state has its probate processes, which dictate how estates are administered and how trusts are executed. Some states have streamlined probate processes that are less cumbersome, while others impose detailed requirements that can prolong estate settlement. If your trust isn't compliant with the local probate laws, you could face unexpected legal hurdles that complicate or delay the distribution of your assets.

Additionally, state differences in estate tax regulations must be considered. While some states impose estate taxes that could affect your estate's value, others do not. This variation can have a substantial impact on the overall tax liabilities your estate will face. For example, if you originally set up your trust in a state with no estate tax and then relocate to one where estate taxes are levied, failing to adjust your trust to account for this could lead to unnecessary tax burdens. Understanding these tax implications is crucial for ensuring that your estate plan remains effective and that your heirs receive the maximum benefit from your assets.

Relocating to a different state introduces another layer of complexity in maintaining compliance with trust laws. When you move, it's essential to seek legal advice to understand how your new state's laws differ from those of your previous state. This guidance is invaluable in identifying necessary adjustments to your trust terms to ensure they align with local regulations. Changes might include updating the trustee, modifying asset distribution terms, or addressing state-specific tax laws. Without these modifications, you risk having aspects of your trust invalidated or facing legal challenges that could disrupt your estate plan.

To stay informed about state-specific requirements, several strategies can be employed. Consulting with local estate planning attorneys is one of the most effective ways to ensure your trust remains compliant. These professionals possess in-depth knowledge of state laws and can provide tailored advice to align your trust with current regulations.

Additionally, utilizing state government resources, such as websites and publications, can offer valuable insights into local trust laws and requirements. These resources often provide official guidelines and updates, helping you stay abreast of any legislative changes that might impact your trust.

Consider the example of a trust requiring modification due to state tax changes. Suppose you initially set up your trust in a state with favorable tax laws, but after relocating, you discover that your new state's tax code imposes additional estate taxes. Without adjusting your trust to reflect these changes, your estate could face unexpected liabilities, reducing the inheritance left to your beneficiaries. In another scenario, differing probate procedures could affect trust execution. Imagine moving to a state with more stringent probate requirements; without adapting your trust to meet these new standards, you might encounter delays in asset distribution, causing frustration for your heirs.

Understanding and adapting to state-specific trust laws is a critical component of effective trust management. By recognizing the variations in probate processes and estate tax regulations and by seeking expert guidance when relocating, you can ensure your trust remains compliant and effective. This awareness not only protects your assets from potential legal challenges but also provides peace of mind, knowing that your estate plan will be executed as intended, regardless of where you live.

Emerging Trends in Estate Planning

The landscape of estate planning is evolving rapidly, influenced by innovative developments that reshape how we manage and secure our assets. One significant trend is the rise of digital estate planning tools. These platforms simplify the process, allowing you to manage your estate from anywhere with an internet connection.

With user-friendly interfaces, these tools enable you to draft and update documents with ease, offering real-time collaboration with your legal advisors. This digital shift also includes the incorporation of digital assets into trusts, ensuring your online presence, from cryptocurrencies to social media accounts, is managed according to your wishes. As more of our lives exist online, these tools provide a comprehensive approach to estate planning, ensuring nothing is overlooked.

Technology plays a pivotal role in modern trust management, enhancing efficiency and accessibility. Online trust management platforms are increasingly popular, offering centralized locations to oversee your entire estate. These platforms allow for seamless communication between trustees and beneficiaries, providing transparent updates and reports. They also enable the integration of digital assets into your trust, ensuring that these modern forms of wealth are protected and distributed according to your wishes. For instance, including cryptocurrencies in your trust can be straightforward with these tools, allowing for secure tracking and management. As digital estates grow, these platforms simplify the process, ensuring your assets are well-managed and easily accessible to those you designate.

Another emerging trend is the focus on sustainability and ethical investing, which is changing how we approach trust asset management. More individuals are choosing to align their investments with personal values, integrating Environmental, Social, and Governance (ESG) criteria into their portfolios. This approach not only reflects a commitment to ethical principles but also responds to a growing demand for responsible investing. By incorporating ESG criteria, you can ensure that your trust's investments support sustainable practices, contributing positively to society and the environment. This trend highlights a shift towards using wealth as a tool for positive impact, making your estate plan a reflection of your values and beliefs.

Consider a trust utilizing blockchain technology for secure asset tracking. Blockchain provides a decentralized, tamper-proof ledger that records transactions transparently. By integrating this technology into your trust, you can enhance security and reduce the risk of fraud. Blockchain's immutable nature ensures that once a transaction is recorded, it cannot be altered, providing a reliable history of asset transfers.

This technology offers a level of transparency and security previously unattainable, making it an attractive option for modern estate planning. Similarly, a scenario involving green investments in a family trust exemplifies the shift towards sustainability. By investing in renewable energy projects or companies with strong ESG commitments, your trust not only supports environmentally conscious initiatives but also potentially benefits from the financial growth associated with these sectors. This alignment of investments with values is becoming a cornerstone of forward-thinking estate planning, reflecting a broader societal trend toward sustainability and ethical responsibility.

These emerging trends in estate planning highlight the importance of staying informed and adaptable. As technology advances and societal values shift, integrating these elements into your trust can ensure it remains relevant and effective. Whether through digital tools, sustainable investing, or cutting-edge technologies like blockchain, embracing these innovations can enhance your estate plan, providing security and alignment with your principles.

By understanding and incorporating these developments, you can create a trust that not only protects your assets but also reflects your legacy and values in today's rapidly changing world.

How to Adjust for Life Changes in Your Trust

Imagine your trust as a living document, one that breathes and evolves alongside your life. This adaptability is crucial because life, as we know, is filled with unexpected turns. Whether it's the joyous arrival of a new child or the complexities of a marital change, your trust needs to reflect these pivotal moments. Think of it as ensuring your trust stays in tune with your current reality. The birth or adoption of a child, for instance, is a momentous occasion that calls for immediate attention to your trust. You would want to ensure that this new family member is included as a beneficiary, securing their future within your estate plan.

On the other hand, a change in marital status, whether through marriage or divorce, often demands a reevaluation of your trust terms. A new marriage might mean adding a spouse as a beneficiary or even as a co-trustee. At the same time, a divorce could lead to their removal from your estate planning documents entirely.

Implementing these changes requires a clear strategy. Begin by updating your beneficiary designations, ensuring that each new addition or removal is accurately reflected in your trust. This step is crucial in safeguarding against future disputes or misunderstandings among family members. Next, consider revising trustee appointments if necessary. For example, a divorce might necessitate the appointment of a new trustee who is impartial and aligned with your current wishes. This ensures that the administration of your trust remains smooth and uncontested. It's also wise to consult with an estate planning attorney during these times to guide you through the legal intricacies of making these adjustments. Their expertise can prove invaluable in ensuring that all changes are legally sound and reflective of your intentions.

Communication plays a pivotal role in managing these transitions effectively. Open dialogue with all stakeholders helps in mitigating potential conflicts and ensures everyone is on the same page. It's crucial to notify beneficiaries of any changes, offering transparency and clarity regarding their roles and expectations. Engaging trustees in the decision-making process is equally important. Their involvement not only fosters trust but also ensures they are fully aware of their responsibilities and the dynamics at play. This collaborative approach can prevent future misunderstandings and promote a harmonious execution of your estate plan.

Consider a scenario where a trust successfully accommodates a new marriage. Suppose an individual marries and wishes to include their spouse in the trust, both as a beneficiary and a trustee. By clearly outlining the spouse's role and sharing within the trust, the individual ensures that their new partner is integrated seamlessly into their estate plan. This proactive adjustment not only secures the spouse's future but also strengthens the trust's structure, reflecting the current family dynamics. In another instance, imagine a trust restructuring after a divorce. An individual might decide to remove their ex-spouse from the trust, appointing a sibling or a close friend as the new trustee. This change not only aligns the trust with the individual's current wishes but also minimizes the risk of future conflicts, providing a fresh start and a clear path forward.

These examples highlight the importance of flexibility and adaptability in trust management. Life changes are inevitable, and your trust should be a reflection of your evolving circumstances. By embracing change and taking proactive steps to adjust your trust, you ensure that your estate plan remains relevant, effective, and aligned with your vision for the future.

Monitoring Trust Performance and Compliance

Maintaining a living trust is not a set-it-and-forget-it task; it requires ongoing oversight to ensure it remains effective and aligned with your goals. Regular assessments of trust performance are crucial for evaluating how well your trust is functioning. Consider it akin to a routine health check for your financial legacy. Start by reviewing asset management strategies.

Are your investments performing as expected? Are they aligned with your risk tolerance and financial objectives? This evaluation can reveal whether current strategies are yielding the desired returns or if adjustments are necessary. Equally important is assessing beneficiary satisfaction. Keeping open lines of communication with beneficiaries can provide insight into their needs and expectations, ensuring the trust continues to serve its intended purpose.

A well-managed trust should meet the needs of both the grantor and the beneficiaries, striking a balance between preserving assets and making necessary distributions.

Compliance plays a pivotal role in trust management, ensuring adherence to both legal and fiduciary standards. Your trust must operate within the framework of the law, adhering to its terms and keeping pace with any changes in legal requirements. This compliance involves regular reviews of the trust document to ensure it reflects current laws and your wishes. It's about keeping abreast of legal shifts that could impact your trust, such as changes in tax law or estate regulations. Failing to comply with these standards can lead to complications, including legal disputes or financial penalties. Staying informed and proactive in maintaining compliance ensures that your trust operates smoothly and remains a reliable tool for managing your estate.

Effective monitoring of your trust's performance and compliance involves employing various tools and techniques. Financial audits are one such tool, providing a comprehensive review of your trust's financial health. These audits can highlight areas of strength and identify potential weaknesses, offering a roadmap for improvement.

Establishing performance benchmarks is another strategy, setting clear goals for asset growth, risk management, and beneficiary satisfaction. These benchmarks serve as a guide for evaluating trust performance and making informed decisions about necessary changes. By leveraging these tools, you can maintain a clear view of your trust's effectiveness and ensure it continues to meet your long-term objectives.

Take the example of a periodic trust audit revealing areas for improvement. Imagine a trust that consistently performs below expectations in terms of investment returns. A thorough audit might uncover that the asset allocation is too conservative, limiting growth potential. Armed with this insight, you can work with your financial advisor to adjust the investment strategy, aligning it more closely with your goals.

In another scenario, beneficiary feedback could inform trust adjustments. Suppose beneficiaries express concerns about the frequency or size of distributions. Engaging in open dialogue can lead to a better understanding of their needs and result in adjustments to the trust terms that enhance satisfaction while preserving the trust's integrity.

Monitoring the performance and compliance of your trust is an ongoing process, essential for ensuring it remains effective and aligned with your goals. By regularly assessing asset management strategies and beneficiary satisfaction, you can maintain a trust that continues to serve your needs.

Compliance with legal standards is equally crucial, requiring diligence and proactive management. Utilizing tools like financial audits and performance benchmarks provides valuable insights into your trust's health, guiding necessary adjustments. Through these practices, you can ensure that your trust remains a robust and reliable tool for managing your estate, providing peace of mind and security for you and your beneficiaries.

Resources for Staying Informed and Up-to-Date

Staying informed about the latest developments and best practices in estate planning is vital for maintaining an effective trust.

One of the most accessible resources for continuous learning is estate planning seminars and workshops. These events bring together experts who share insights and strategies, providing a platform for learning and networking. Attending such seminars allows you to hear firsthand from professionals about new trends, legal changes, and innovative tools that can enhance your trust management. Workshops often offer interactive sessions where you can engage directly with the material, gaining practical skills that can be applied to your trust.

In addition to in-person events, online courses, and webinars have become invaluable tools for staying current. They offer the flexibility to learn at your own pace, either from the comfort of your home or on the go. These digital resources cover a wide range of topics, from basic estate planning principles to advanced trust management strategies. Webinars often feature live Q&A sessions with experts, allowing you to clarify doubts and gain deeper insights into specific areas of interest. This format is particularly useful for tackling complex topics, as you can revisit the material as needed, ensuring a thorough understanding.

Professional advisors play a crucial role in staying informed and adapting to changes in the estate planning landscape. Regular consultations with estate planning attorneys provide tailored guidance, ensuring your trust remains aligned with current laws and regulations. These professionals can offer insights into new legal developments and suggest adjustments to your trust that reflect these changes. Similarly, financial advisors are essential for navigating market trends and economic shifts. They can help you refine your investment strategies, ensuring your trust's assets are managed effectively to meet your financial goals. By maintaining a strong relationship with these advisors, you benefit from their expertise and experience, which can significantly enhance your trust management.

Technology also offers a wealth of resources for staying informed. Subscribing to estate planning newsletters is a simple yet effective way to receive regular updates on the latest news and trends. These publications typically include articles by experts highlighting key issues and offering practical advice. Engaging with online forums and community groups provides a platform for sharing experiences and learning from others in similar situations. These forums often host discussions on recent legal changes, innovative strategies, and common challenges, offering a supportive environment where you can learn and contribute.

Consider the case of a family that effectively utilizes online platforms for trust management updates. They subscribe to estate planning newsletters, which inform them of changes in tax laws and provide tips for optimizing their trust. By participating in online forums, they gain insights into how other families manage similar trusts, allowing them to adapt successful strategies to their situation. The family also attends regular webinars, where they learn about emerging trends and tools, keeping their trust management approach up-to-date and effective. This proactive engagement with digital resources ensures their trust remains robust and aligned with their goals.

Another example involves leveraging professional networks for estate planning insights. A business owner regularly consults with a team of advisors, including an estate planning attorney and a financial advisor. This collaboration enables the owner to stay informed about legal developments and market trends, ensuring their trust reflects the latest best practices. By attending industry seminars and workshops, the owner further deepens their understanding of trust management, gaining new perspectives that inform their decisions.

This comprehensive approach to education and resource utilization empowers the owner to manage their trust confidently, knowing it is well-positioned to achieve their objectives. Incorporating these resources into your trust management strategy ensures you remain informed and adaptable in an ever-changing landscape.

By actively engaging with educational opportunities, leveraging professional guidance, and utilizing digital tools, you maintain a trust that is both resilient and effective. These efforts not only enhance your trust management capabilities but also provide peace of mind, knowing that your estate plan is current and aligned with your intentions. As we close this chapter, consider how these resources can support your ongoing commitment to maintaining and updating your trust, ensuring it continues to serve the needs of both you and your beneficiaries. Moving forward, we will explore the intricacies of crafting a legacy that extends beyond financial wealth, delving into the meaningful impact you can create through thoughtful estate planning.

Addressing Common Concerns and FAQs

Imagine sitting at your kitchen table, a steaming cup of coffee in hand, as you ponder the possibility of creating a living trust. You've heard the buzz about how it can protect your assets and provide peace of mind, but you're also wary of the costs and complexities. The question looms: should you do it yourself or enlist the help of a professional? This chapter unravels that dilemma, offering a clear path through the maze of estate planning decisions.

Do I Need a Lawyer? DIY vs. Professional Help

The allure of crafting a living trust on your own can be tempting. After all, the internet is awash with resources promising to guide you through the process at a fraction of the cost of hiring a lawyer. For those with straightforward estates, this DIY approach can indeed be cost-effective.

You might spend under $100, making it an attractive option for individuals who want to sidestep the higher fees associated with legal services. Online platforms offer templates and step-by-step instructions, simplifying what once seemed daunting. However, the devil, as they say, is in the details. While you might save money upfront, there's a risk of making technical errors or omitting crucial documents, which can render your trust invalid and lead to costly disputes down the line.

In contrast, professional assistance provides a safety net of expertise, particularly vital for complex estate structures or when navigating the labyrinth of state-specific laws. An attorney's guidance ensures that your trust is tailored to your unique needs and complies with all legal requirements. This is especially crucial if your estate involves multiple properties, business interests, or blended family dynamics. A professional can help you develop a comprehensive estate plan that not only addresses current laws but also anticipates future changes, providing peace of mind that your assets will be managed as intended. Moreover, lawyers can offer strategic advice on asset protection and tax optimization, which is essential for high-net-worth individuals seeking to maximize their estate's efficiency.

Technology has ushered in a new era of accessibility, offering hybrid solutions that blend the DIY approach with professional oversight. Many legal services now operate online, providing document preparation and virtual consultations that bridge the gap between doing it yourself and hiring a lawyer. These platforms cater to those who prefer the convenience of digital tools while still valuing expert input. They offer a middle ground, allowing you to draft documents online and then have a professional review them for accuracy and compliance. This approach can be a cost-effective compromise, ensuring your trust is legally sound without the full expense of traditional legal services.

Consider the scenario of a young couple, Mark and Lisa, who chose to set up a straightforward family trust using an online platform. Their estate comprised a single property and modest savings, making the DIY route feasible. The platform provided them with templates and a checklist, ensuring they captured all necessary details.

After completing the documents, they opted for a virtual consultation to review their work, gaining confidence that their trust was correctly structured. Alternatively, imagine a seasoned entrepreneur, Jonathan, whose estate includes multiple businesses and investments. Recognizing the complexity of his situation, he engaged an estate planning attorney to craft a bespoke plan. The lawyer's expertise ensured that Jonathan's assets were protected from creditors and that his trust included provisions for business succession, reflecting his vision for the future.

Reflection Section: Choosing Your Path

- **Simple Estates**: Consider a DIY approach if your estate is straightforward and you feel comfortable with online tools.

- **Complex Estates**: Seek professional assistance if your estate involves intricate structures or you wish to optimize for taxes.

- **Hybrid Approach**: Utilize online platforms with professional reviews for a balanced solution.

Choosing between DIY and professional help ultimately hinges on your estate's complexity and your comfort level with the intricacies of legal documentation. With the right approach, you can create a living trust that safeguards your assets and achieves your estate planning goals.

Understanding Costs: Is It Worth It?

Embarking on the path to establishing a living trust often prompts a critical consideration: the financial commitment involved. The cost of setting up a trust can vary significantly based on several factors, including the complexity of your estate and the approach you choose. If you hire an attorney, fees can range from $1,000 to $4,000, and for complex estates, these costs may exceed $5,000.

This investment covers the attorney's expertise in crafting a tailored trust that aligns with your specific needs and ensures compliance with current laws. On the other hand, opting for a do-it-yourself method can reduce expenses to between $400 and $1,000, but this approach might increase the risk of errors, especially if your estate isn't straightforward. It's important to weigh these initial costs against the potential long-term benefits that a trust offers.

Beyond the setup, ongoing maintenance and administration costs can also impact your financial planning. These might include fees for managing the assets within the trust or paying a trustee if you choose not to take on this role yourself. While these are recurring expenses, they can be viewed as a necessary investment in the seamless management and eventual distribution of your assets.

A well-managed trust can prevent costly legal battles or probate fees, which often consume a substantial portion of an estate. This consideration is especially relevant for those with larger estates, where the savings from avoiding probate can far outweigh the costs of maintaining a trust.

Evaluating whether a trust is worth the investment involves a detailed cost-benefit analysis. The size and complexity of your estate are pivotal factors. Larger estates or those with diverse assets, such as businesses or multiple properties, can benefit significantly from the structured management a trust provides. The potential savings from avoiding probate, which can consume 3% to 8% of the estate's value, are a compelling reason to consider a trust. Trusts can also offer privacy, a valuable asset for those who prefer to keep estate matters confidential. By bypassing the public probate process, trusts ensure that your financial affairs remain private, shielded from public scrutiny.

The long-term financial impacts of establishing a trust can be substantial. Trusts preserve the estate's value by ensuring a smooth transfer of assets, minimizing the risk of disputes that might erode the estate's worth. They also offer tax advantages that contribute to financial stability over time. For instance, irrevocable trusts can reduce estate taxes by removing assets from the taxable estate, providing more for your beneficiaries.

This strategic financial planning can enhance the legacy you leave behind, ensuring that your heirs benefit from the full value of your estate. It's a proactive approach to safeguarding your wealth and supporting your loved ones' futures.

Consider the case of a large estate, where the decedent's assets included multiple properties and a thriving business. By setting up a trust, the estate avoided the prolonged and costly probate process, allowing beneficiaries to access their inheritance quickly. The trust also included provisions for business succession, ensuring the continued success of the family business. On the other hand, picture a smaller estate where the family initially hesitated to incur the costs of professional services. However, they eventually realized that the expense of probate, both in terms of time and money, far surpassed the investment in setting up and maintaining a trust. This realization prompted them to seek professional guidance, ultimately saving the estate from potential legal challenges and ensuring a smoother asset distribution.

These scenarios illustrate the diverse financial outcomes a trust can offer, reinforcing the importance of weighing costs against the benefits of financial security and peace of mind.

How to Protect Your Family from Disputes

Imagine the Smith family, who thought they had everything sorted when their parents passed away. It quickly became apparent that the distribution of their estate was not as straightforward as they had believed. The siblings found themselves at odds over what they perceived as unequal asset distribution. Such situations are common triggers for disputes.

An unequal distribution can feel like a personal slight, especially if one sibling perceives that another has been favored. Ambiguities in the terms of trust can exacerbate these feelings, leaving room for varied interpretations and misunderstandings. The Smiths are not alone in this; many families face friction when the language of a trust document isn't crystal clear.

To minimize the risk of such conflicts, open and honest communication is key. The more transparent you are about your intentions, the less room there is for misinterpretation. Consider regular family meetings where you can discuss the trust's terms and your reasons for specific decisions. This approach helps set expectations and provides a forum for family members to voice concerns or ask questions. When everyone understands the rationale behind asset distribution, it becomes easier to accept, even if it's not exactly what they hoped for. Such discussions also offer the chance to make alterations while you're still able, ensuring the trust reflects your current wishes and those of your family.

Mediation and conflict resolution can serve as valuable tools when disputes seem inevitable. A neutral third party can facilitate discussions, helping everyone reach a consensus without the emotional weight that family dynamics often bring. Professional mediation services offer structured environments where each party can express their views and work toward a mutually agreeable solution. In some cases, conflict resolution workshops can equip your family with the skills needed to handle disagreements constructively.

These workshops teach techniques for effective communication and problem-solving, fostering a cooperative spirit that can be invaluable in tense situations.

Consider the story of the Johnsons, who successfully navigated a potential dispute with the help of mediation. The family was struggling with differing opinions on how to divide a vacation property that held sentimental value. A mediator helped them explore various options, ultimately leading to an agreement that satisfied everyone involved.

Similarly, the Browns, a family of four siblings, found themselves at odds over their late mother's estate. With the help of facilitated discussions, they reached a consensus on asset distribution, preserving their relationships in the process.

These examples highlight the potential for positive outcomes when families proactively address disputes and seek professional guidance. By fostering an environment of openness and understanding, you can protect your family from the discord that estate planning disagreements often bring.

Ensuring Fair Treatment of Blended Families

In the intricate tapestry of blended families, estate planning presents unique challenges that can stir up significant conflict. Imagine a family where biological and stepchildren each hold different expectations about inheritance.

It's not uncommon for stepchildren to fear being overlooked or for biological children to feel entitled to a larger share, especially if they have spent more time with the parent. These differing expectations can lead to disputes that tear at the fabric of family unity. Ensuring equitable treatment of all heirs becomes a tightrope walk, balancing fairness with the realities of family dynamics. This balance is crucial to maintaining peace and ensuring that everyone feels valued and respected within the family structure.

To navigate these challenges, strategic planning is crucial. One effective approach is creating separate trusts for different family branches. This allows for a clear delineation of assets, ensuring that each branch of the family receives what is deemed fair without stepping on one another's toes. For instance, a separate trust for biological children can contain assets that have sentimental value or direct lineage. In contrast, another trust for stepchildren includes assets allocated with their needs and contributions in mind.

Additionally, life insurance can be a powerful tool to equalize inheritances. It can provide a financial cushion that ensures no child feels shortchanged, thereby preventing potential disputes. This strategy often proves invaluable in balancing interests and fostering a sense of equality among all family members.

Open dialogue forms the backbone of successful estate planning in blended families. Regular family meetings offer a platform to discuss estate plans transparently, helping to align everyone's expectations and reduce misunderstandings. In these meetings, discussing the rationale behind decisions openly can demystify the planning process, turning potential points of contention into opportunities for understanding. Written agreements further solidify these discussions, providing a tangible reference that outlines each party's intentions and expectations.

These documents act as a safeguard, preventing future disputes by clearly delineating what was agreed upon. This transparency not only aids in conflict prevention but also builds trust among family members, paving the way for harmonious relationships.

Consider the example of the Anderson family, who navigated their complex dynamics by setting up a trust that included provisions for both biological and stepchildren. They engaged in open discussions, ensuring everyone understood the reasoning behind each decision. This approach fostered a spirit of cooperation and mutual respect, allowing them to craft a plan that felt fair to all involved. Similarly, the Martinez family faced a potential minefield of conflicts. By enlisting the help of professional advisors, they were able to navigate these complexities with a clear strategy. The advisors helped them create a detailed plan that addressed each family member's unique needs, resulting in an estate plan that was both comprehensive and considerate.

Through clear communication and expert guidance, both families managed to create estate plans that honored each member, illustrating the effectiveness of thoughtful planning in blended families.

Clarifying Misconceptions: What's True and What's Not

Living trusts often carry an air of mystique, shrouded in misconceptions that can deter people from exploring their potential. A prevailing myth is that trusts are exclusively for the wealthy, a notion that roots itself in the complex history of estate planning.

It's easy to understand why this belief persists. Trusts have long been associated with sprawling estates and high-net-worth individuals. However, this is a misconception that can limit the financial strategies of middle-income families.

Trusts are not reserved for the elite. They provide a flexible tool for anyone looking to manage their assets more effectively. The reality is that trusts offer benefits like avoiding probate, which can be costly and time-consuming, regardless of the size of one's estate. By bypassing probate, families can save money and time, making trusts a practical choice for many.

Another common misunderstanding is about the revocability of trusts. Some people believe that once they set up a trust, they lose all control over its terms and assets. This confusion often stems from the mix-up between revocable and irrevocable trusts. A revocable trust, as its name suggests, offers tremendous flexibility. You retain the ability to alter or even dismantle it entirely if your circumstances change. This feature makes it an appealing option for those who anticipate life changes and want to maintain control over their assets.

On the other hand, irrevocable trusts, once established, cannot be easily changed. They serve different purposes, such as providing asset protection and tax benefits. Understanding these distinctions is crucial for choosing the right trust for your needs.

These misconceptions often arise from unreliable sources. Misleading advice can spread easily, especially when it comes from unqualified individuals or outdated media. The internet, while a valuable resource, is filled with content that isn't always accurate.

People may stumble upon forums or articles that perpetuate myths, inadvertently steering them away from beneficial financial planning tools. It's crucial to seek information from reputable sources, such as estate planning professionals or verified publications. Keeping up with current estate planning practices can also help dispel outdated beliefs, ensuring that your decisions are informed and effective.

Consider the case of the Thompsons, a moderate-income family who initially dismissed the idea of a trust due to perceived complexity and cost. After consulting a financial advisor, they learned about the probate-avoiding benefits of a living trust. They decided to set one up, which allowed them to streamline their estate management and avoid unnecessary legal fees. This decision proved advantageous, as it provided peace of mind and financial savings. In another instance, a client misunderstood the flexibility of a revocable trust. She thought establishing one would mean losing control over her assets, but after a detailed discussion with her attorney, she realized she could make changes as needed. This newfound understanding prompted her to create a revocable trust, giving her the confidence to manage her estate proactively. These examples highlight how dispelling myths can lead to more informed and beneficial estate planning decisions.

Frequently Asked Questions: Quick Answers

Living trusts often raise a flurry of questions for those new to estate planning. A common inquiry is, "How does a living trust differ from a will?" While both serve as estate planning tools, they function differently. A will outlines how your assets should be distributed after your death and becomes effective only upon your passing. It must go through probate, a court-supervised process that can take time and money, which also exposes the will to public scrutiny. In contrast, a living trust is effective immediately upon creation, allowing you to manage your assets during your lifetime and avoid probate altogether. This means your estate can be distributed more quickly and privately without the need for court intervention.

Another frequent question is, "What happens if I don't update my trust regularly?" Not updating your trust can lead to unintended consequences. Life changes—such as marriage, divorce, the birth of a child, or even changes in state laws—can render your current trust outdated. An outdated trust might not reflect your current wishes or accommodate new family members, creating confusion and potential disputes among beneficiaries. Regular updates ensure that your trust accurately represents your intentions and adheres to the latest legal requirements. This practice not only secures your assets but also prevents complications that could arise from ambiguous or outdated terms.

Embracing the importance of ongoing education in estate planning cannot be overstated. As laws and circumstances evolve, keeping informed about these changes is crucial. Consider tapping into resources for further exploration. Books, webinars, and online courses offer a wealth of knowledge that can deepen your understanding of estate planning. Consulting with professionals is also invaluable, especially when dealing with complex issues that require specialized legal advice. Their expertise can provide clarity and guidance, ensuring your estate plan remains robust and effective in achieving your goals.

To illustrate these points, consider the story of the Peterson family. They initially believed that a simple will was sufficient for their needs, only to face a prolonged probate process that delayed the distribution of their assets. This experience highlighted the advantages of a living trust, prompting them to establish one to avoid similar delays in the future. In another scenario, a family neglected to update their trust after a significant life event. This oversight resulted in the exclusion of a new family member from the estate plan, leading to disputes and legal challenges. These examples underscore the importance of understanding and maintaining an up-to-date estate plan.

As we wrap up this chapter, remember that estate planning is an ongoing process. It requires diligence, adaptability, and a willingness to learn. By equipping yourself with the right knowledge and tools, you can create a living trust that not only protects your assets but also ensures your legacy is preserved according to your wishes. In the upcoming chapter, we'll explore advanced strategies for maximizing the benefits of your estate plan, delving into techniques that can enhance your financial security and provide lasting peace of mind.

Empowering Self-Education and Legacy Building

Imagine sitting in your favorite chair, a cup of coffee steaming beside you, as you leaf through a well-worn book on estate planning. The margins are filled with notes, and the pages are dog-eared from frequent use. This is your guide, your compass, as you navigate the sometimes murky waters of estate planning. Many people, like you, are finding empowerment in taking control of their financial futures through self-education. By understanding the intricacies of legal and financial concepts, you can make informed decisions that align with your goals and protect your legacy. This knowledge transforms what might seem like an overwhelming task into one of empowerment and confidence.

In our interconnected world, the resources available for self-education are vast and varied. Online courses and webinars offer the convenience of learning at your own pace, providing expert insights into the nuances of estate planning. Websites like Coursera and Udemy host courses tailored to different levels of understanding, from beginner to advanced. Books and guides, both digital and physical, continue to be invaluable. Titles such as "Estate Planning Basics" and "The Complete Book of Wills and Estates" offer comprehensive overviews and practical advice. For those who prefer listening, podcasts and audiobooks bring expert voices into your living room or car. These resources, easily accessible and often free or low-cost, empower you to build a solid foundation of knowledge.

Lifelong learning is not just a buzzword but a necessity in the ever-evolving landscape of estate management. Laws change, financial markets fluctuate, and what worked yesterday might not be effective tomorrow. Staying informed about these shifts ensures that your estate plan remains relevant and effective. Keeping up with legal amendments, such as changes in tax laws or probate regulations, can prevent unforeseen complications. Similarly, understanding financial market trends helps in making strategic investment decisions that safeguard your assets. Engaging with current events through reputable news sources or professional journals keeps you at the forefront of these changes, allowing you to adapt your strategies as needed.

Consider the story of Jane, a retiree who, after her husband's passing, decided to take charge of her estate planning. Despite having limited financial knowledge, Jane embraced self-education with determination. She attended local workshops, read extensively on the subject, and consulted online resources. Her diligence paid off, as she successfully crafted a comprehensive estate plan that protected her assets and provided for her grandchildren's education. Jane's experience is a testament to the power of self-education in transforming uncertainty into empowerment. Similarly, Tom, a young professional, realized the importance of securing his financial future early on. Through online courses and careful study, Tom gained the skills and confidence to manage his investments and plan his estate effectively, ensuring peace of mind for his future family.

Resource List: Tools for Self-Education

- **Online Courses and Webinars**: Explore platforms like Coursera, Udemy, and edX for tailored estate planning courses.
- **Books and Guides**: Consider reading "Estate Planning Basics" by Denis Clifford and "The Complete Book of Wills and Estates" by Alexander A. Bove Jr.
- **Podcasts and Audiobooks**: Listen to estate planning podcasts and audiobooks for expert insights on the go.
- **Local Workshops and Seminars**: Attend community events for hands-on learning and networking opportunities.
- **Professional Journals and News Sources**: Stay updated on legal and financial trends through reputable publications.

These stories and resources illustrate that anyone, regardless of their starting point, can become proficient in estate planning. By taking an active role in your education, you gain not only valuable skills but also the confidence to make decisions that reflect your values and aspirations.

Interactive Tools for Ongoing Learning

Imagine estate planning as a dynamic puzzle, one that constantly changes as pieces are added or removed. Interactive tools can be invaluable to keep up with this evolving landscape. Digital resources like apps specifically designed for estate planning management make this process more accessible. These apps offer features such as real-time tracking of your trust's performance, alerts for important deadlines, and even the ability to simulate different scenarios to understand potential outcomes. App interfaces are usually user-friendly, often breaking down complex tasks into manageable actions, allowing you to focus on what's important without getting bogged down by minutiae. They serve as a personal assistant, reminding you when it's time to review your estate documents or when a law change might affect your plan.

Interactive workshops and simulations offer another layer of engagement. These platforms enable you to step into hypothetical scenarios, testing how different decisions might impact your estate. Imagine participating in a virtual workshop where you simulate the effects of various investment strategies on your trust's growth or explore the potential impact of different tax scenarios on your estate's value. This hands-on experience can demystify complex concepts, making them more tangible and easier to grasp. Through simulations, you not only learn the theory but also see its practical implications, enhancing your understanding and retention of the material. This method of learning caters to different styles, allowing you to choose scenarios that align with your specific interests and needs.

Effectively integrating these tools into your daily planning requires a strategic approach. Start by setting up regular reminders on your app to prompt you to review and update your estate plan periodically. This ensures that your plan remains aligned with your current circumstances and goals. Use simulations to explore different planning scenarios, such as the financial implications of a new investment or the impact of gifting assets to family members. By regularly engaging with these tools, you create a habit of proactive management, ensuring that estate planning becomes a seamless part of your routine rather than a daunting task you face only during major life events.

The advantages of interactive learning extend beyond mere convenience. They foster greater engagement, as the active participation required in simulations and workshops makes the learning process more memorable. By interacting with the material, you develop a deeper understanding, which in turn boosts your confidence in making informed decisions. Interactive tools also offer personalized learning paths, allowing you to tailor your educational experience to your unique needs and interests. This customization ensures that you focus on areas most relevant to your estate planning journey, maximizing the value you derive from these resources.

Consider a family using an estate planning app to track their trust's performance. They receive notifications about market changes that could affect their investments, allowing them to adjust their strategy accordingly. This proactive approach ensures they stay ahead of potential challenges, safeguarding their financial legacy. Similarly, imagine a virtual workshop where participants engage in estate planning simulations. They explore the effects of different retirement strategies, gaining insights that inform their future decisions. These examples highlight how interactive tools can transform estate planning from a static task into a dynamic, engaging process that empowers you to take control of your financial future.

Planning for a Digital Legacy

In today's interconnected world, the concept of a digital legacy has taken on new significance. Just as we manage our physical assets, the digital footprints we leave behind require thoughtful planning. This encompasses everything from your social media profiles to the digital currency stored in virtual wallets.

Managing these assets ensures that your online identity reflects your wishes even after you're gone. It's about preserving personal memories, like family photos stored online, and managing valuable digital assets, such as cryptocurrencies or domain names that hold financial worth. As we increasingly live our lives in the digital realm, the need to incorporate these elements into our estate planning becomes not just important but necessary.

Creating a digital legacy plan involves several actionable steps to ensure your digital affairs are in order. Begin by cataloging your online accounts, from email and social media to banking and subscriptions. Please make a list of usernames and passwords, but store them securely to protect against unauthorized access. Designating a digital executor, someone you trust to manage these accounts, is another crucial step.

This individual should have clear instructions for handling your digital assets, whether it involves memorializing a social media profile or transferring ownership of digital files. It's about ensuring that your digital presence is handled respectfully and in accordance with your wishes, preventing the chaos that can ensue without a clear plan.

Legal considerations play a significant role in digital legacy planning. Digital rights laws vary widely, and navigating these can be complex. Each digital platform has its terms of service, which can dictate how accounts are handled after death. Some platforms allow for account memorialization, while others may require a court order to access or transfer account ownership. Compliance with these terms is essential to ensure your digital executor can carry out your wishes without legal hurdles. Consulting with an attorney who specializes in digital estate planning can provide valuable guidance, helping you to create a legally sound plan that respects both your rights and the policies of the platforms you use.

Consider the story of Lisa, a professional photographer who built her career around a vast digital portfolio. To ensure her work continued to inspire, she meticulously documented her digital assets, including cloud storage access and editing software licenses. She named a trusted colleague as her digital executor, providing detailed instructions for managing her portfolio. This not only preserved her artistic legacy but also provided ongoing income for her family through licensing agreements.

Similarly, think of Sam, who invested heavily in cryptocurrency. By including detailed instructions in his digital estate plan, he ensured that his digital assets would be transferred seamlessly to his heirs, avoiding potential legal challenges and financial loss.

These examples highlight the crucial role digital legacy planning plays in protecting both personal and financial interests. Creating a digital legacy plan is an act of foresight that respects the digital landscape we now inhabit. It's a way to ensure that your digital identity, from cherished memories to valuable assets, is managed according to your wishes, providing peace of mind for you and clarity for those you leave behind.

Building a Legacy: More Than Just Assets

A legacy extends far beyond the tangible value of financial wealth. It encompasses the intangible elements that define who you are and what you stand for. Consider the rich tapestry of family traditions and stories passed down through generations.

These narratives, filled with lessons and experiences, form the core of your personal history and identity. They offer wisdom to future generations, teaching them resilience, love, and the importance of family bonds. When crafting your legacy, think about how you wish to be remembered and how your values can continue to influence and inspire long after you are gone.

Beyond memories and traditions, establishing charitable foundations or scholarships can be a powerful way to ensure that your impact endures. By supporting causes that resonate with your values, you extend your influence into the future, fostering change and growth in areas that matter to you. Whether funding educational opportunities or supporting community projects, these initiatives become a testament to your commitment to making the world a better place. Your legacy becomes a beacon of hope and inspiration, encouraging others to contribute and carry forward your vision.

Aligning your estate planning with your personal beliefs involves deliberate and thoughtful strategies. Creating an ethical will is one such method. Unlike a traditional will, which distributes assets, an ethical will conveys your values, hopes, and dreams to your loved ones. It's a heartfelt letter that offers guidance and reflection, providing insight into what truly matters to you.

Another strategy is to establish a family mission statement. This declaration encapsulates your family's values and goals, setting a clear path for current and future generations to follow. It serves as a guiding light, ensuring that your family's legacy remains cohesive and aligned with your core beliefs.

Philanthropy can play a significant role in building a meaningful legacy. Charitable giving not only benefits the recipients but also enriches the giver, creating a cycle of generosity and goodwill. By setting up donor-advised funds, you can manage your charitable contributions flexibly, choosing which causes to support and involving your family in these decisions.

This collaborative approach fosters a sense of unity and shared purpose, reinforcing your family's values. Creating endowments for causes you care about ensures sustained impact, providing ongoing support and growth for initiatives close to your heart. Your legacy thus becomes a living entity, continually evolving and adapting to the needs of the world.

Consider the story of the Patel family, who established a foundation to support educational initiatives in underserved communities. Their vision was to provide resources and opportunities for children to succeed, regardless of their circumstances. Through scholarships and mentorship programs, they created a ripple effect, transforming lives and inspiring future generations to pursue their dreams.

Similarly, the Ortega family launched a legacy project aimed at preserving their cultural heritage. By funding a community center and cultural programs, they ensured that their traditions and history remained vibrant and accessible, fostering pride and connection among their descendants.

Each of these examples showcases the profound impact of thoughtful legacy planning that goes beyond mere financial wealth. These stories demonstrate that a legacy isn't simply about the assets you leave behind. It's about the values and beliefs you pass on, the memories you preserve, and the impact you make on the world around you. Your legacy is the culmination of a lifetime of choices, actions, and dreams woven together to create a lasting testament to who you are.

As you consider your legacy, think about the stories you want to tell, the changes you wish to inspire, and the values you hope to instill in those who follow. Your legacy is your gift to the future, a reflection of your life and the enduring impact you have made.

Innovative Approaches to Estate Planning

In recent years, estate planning has seen a technological transformation, offering new and innovative ways to manage and protect your assets.

The advent of blockchain technology has introduced a secure method for handling estate transactions, ensuring transparency and reducing the risk of fraud. Blockchain's decentralized nature means that every transaction is recorded across multiple computers, making it nearly impossible to alter or hack. This technology can revolutionize how real estate deeds are managed within trusts, providing an unprecedented level of security. Imagine a future where the transfer of property is seamless, requiring only a digital transaction verified by a global network, eliminating the need for cumbersome paperwork and reducing the risk of disputes over asset ownership.

Artificial Intelligence (AI) is also playing a pivotal role in modern estate planning by offering personalized advice tailored to your unique circumstances. AI algorithms analyze vast amounts of data quickly, providing insights and recommendations that would take human advisors much longer to generate. These platforms can assess your financial situation, predict future needs, and suggest optimal strategies for asset distribution and tax efficiency.

Whether you're considering philanthropic endeavors or planning for your grandchildren's education, AI-driven tools can help craft a plan that aligns perfectly with your goals and values, ensuring that your estate plan remains robust and adaptable to changing circumstances.

Technology is not just enhancing what we can do with estate planning; it's fundamentally changing the process itself.

Take smart contracts, for instance. These are self-executing contracts with the terms of the agreement directly written into lines of code. They automatically enforce and execute actions like asset transfers when predetermined conditions are met without the need for intermediaries. This automation reduces human error and speeds up transactions, providing peace of mind that your wishes will be carried out precisely as intended.

Additionally, digital vaults offer a secure and convenient way to store and manage your estate documents. These vaults protect sensitive information, ensuring that your important documents are accessible only to those you designate, safeguarding your privacy and security.

Adaptability has become a cornerstone of effective estate planning, especially as new technologies emerge and evolve. Embracing change and innovation means being open to integrating these tools into your estate plan. Flexibility allows you to adjust and refine your strategies, accommodating shifts in the legal landscape or personal circumstances. Continuous learning is essential to leverage these technological advances, ensuring that you stay informed about new developments and opportunities. By doing so, you maintain control over your estate, ensuring that it remains aligned with your intentions and capable of meeting the needs of future generations.

Picture a tech-savvy family utilizing blockchain to manage their real estate assets within a trust. They enjoy the benefits of streamlined transactions and enhanced security, knowing that each property transfer is recorded transparently and permanently. This approach not only simplifies estate management but also reduces legal fees, making the process more efficient and cost-effective. Similarly, consider an individual using an AI-driven platform to receive estate planning insights. The platform assesses their financial portfolio, suggesting strategies to optimize tax savings and ensure a steady income for retirement. By embracing these innovative tools, they create a comprehensive estate plan that adapts to their evolving needs, assuring that their legacy will be preserved.

By understanding and adopting these innovative strategies, you can ensure that your estate planning is not only effective but also future-proof. These tools offer new levels of security, efficiency, and personalization, allowing you to craft a plan that reflects your vision and protects your legacy. As technology continues to advance, the possibilities for enhancing estate planning are limitless, promising a future where managing your estate is as dynamic and adaptable as the world we live in.

Creating a Community of Knowledge and Support

Imagine estate planning not as a solitary task but as a collaborative endeavor enriched by the wisdom and experiences of others. A supportive community can transform the process from daunting to manageable.

When you engage with others who share similar goals, you gain access to a wealth of knowledge that enhances your planning efforts. This exchange of ideas and strategies builds a network of support, providing reassurance and guidance. By participating in discussions, you learn from peers who have faced similar challenges and found effective solutions while also gaining insights from experts who can clarify complex concepts. This collective wisdom empowers you to navigate the intricacies of estate planning with greater confidence and clarity.

Building such a community starts with seeking out forums and groups dedicated to estate planning. Online platforms like Reddit and dedicated Facebook groups offer spaces where individuals come together to ask questions, share experiences, and provide advice. These virtual communities break down geographical barriers, connecting you with diverse perspectives from people around the world. Local workshops and seminars also offer valuable opportunities to engage with others in your area.

These events often feature guest speakers, including estate planning professionals who can provide expert insights and answer questions. Attending these gatherings fosters a sense of camaraderie and shared purpose, creating connections that extend beyond the confines of the meeting room. By actively participating in these communities, you contribute to a culture of learning and mutual support.

Mentorship plays a crucial role in estate planning, offering personalized guidance from those who have successfully navigated the process. Finding a mentor who understands your goals and challenges can provide invaluable insights and motivation. This relationship offers a safe space to ask questions and explore strategies tailored to your unique circumstances. Professional networks, such as local bar associations or financial planning groups, can connect you with experienced individuals willing to share their expertise.

Engaging with these networks not only enhances your understanding but also expands your access to resources and tools that can streamline your planning efforts. With the support of a mentor, you gain a trusted advisor who can help you make informed decisions and avoid potential pitfalls.

Consider the story of a local estate planning group that transformed the experience for its members. By meeting regularly, the group created a supportive environment where members shared updates on their progress, discussed challenges, and celebrated successes. They invited guest speakers to provide insights on topics ranging from tax strategies to digital asset management, enriching their collective knowledge. This community-driven approach empowered individuals to tackle estate planning with renewed confidence, knowing they had a network of support to lean on.

Similarly, an online community dedicated to estate planning became a hub for sharing resources and advice. Members exchanged templates, checklists, and success stories, fostering a sense of camaraderie and cooperation.

Creating a community of knowledge and support is not just about learning; it's about building relationships that foster growth and resilience. By sharing experiences and insights, you contribute to a collective wisdom that benefits everyone involved. In this supportive environment, estate planning becomes less about individual challenges and more about shared goals and solutions.

These examples highlight the transformative power of community-based learning, where collaboration leads to greater understanding and success. Through active participation, you gain access to diverse perspectives, expert advice, and practical tools that enhance your planning efforts.

As you engage with others who share your aspirations, you create a network that empowers you to navigate the complexities of estate planning with confidence and clarity. This collaborative approach transforms estate planning from a solitary task into a shared journey, where the collective wisdom of the community guides you toward achieving your goals.

CONCLUSION

As we come to the end of our journey exploring the world of living trusts, I want to express my gratitude for your dedication and commitment to securing your financial future.

Throughout this book, we've delved into the intricacies of estate planning, uncovering the power of living trusts to protect your assets, avoid probate, and provide lasting peace of mind. By understanding these core concepts and their role in your overall estate plan, you've taken a significant step towards empowering yourself and your loved ones.

Self-education is key to unlocking the full potential of your estate plan. As you continue to learn and explore, you'll gain the confidence to make informed decisions that align with your unique goals and values. Take advantage of available resources, from online courses and workshops to professional advisors who can guide you through the nuances of trust creation and management. Your commitment to ongoing learning will ensure that your estate plan remains robust and adaptable in the face of life's changes.

Remember, your living trust is a dynamic entity that requires regular attention and updates. As laws evolve, your family grows, and your circumstances shift, your trust must adapt to reflect these changes. By regularly reviewing and revising your estate plan, you maintain its effectiveness and relevance. This proactive approach ensures that your wishes are honored and your loved ones are cared for, no matter what the future holds.

As you navigate the complexities of estate planning, don't forget the importance of open and honest communication with your family. By involving your loved ones in the process, you foster a shared understanding of your intentions and values. This collaborative approach not only strengthens family bonds but also ensures a smoother transition when the time comes to implement your estate plan. Transparency and dialogue are essential to maintaining harmony and preventing conflicts.

Your legacy extends far beyond the assets you leave behind. It encompasses the memories you create, the values you instill, and the impact you have on future generations. As you craft your estate plan, consider how you want to be remembered. Incorporate your personal beliefs, philanthropic goals, and the lessons you wish to pass on. By building a comprehensive legacy, you ensure that your influence endures, inspiring and guiding those who follow in your footsteps.

Now is the time to take action. Armed with the knowledge and strategies you've gained from this book, you're ready to embark on your estate planning journey with confidence. Start by reviewing your current plan or initiating the process if you haven't already. Engage with the professionals who can help you navigate the legal and financial landscape. Utilize the tools and resources provided to streamline your efforts and ensure a thorough, well-crafted plan.

As you move forward, remember that you're not alone. Seek out the support and wisdom of others who share your goals and aspirations. Participate in estate planning communities, both online and in-person, where you can learn from experienced individuals and contribute your insights. This collective knowledge and encouragement will be invaluable as you work towards securing your legacy.

Your dedication to understanding living trusts and proactively managing your estate is a testament to your commitment to your loved ones and your financial well-being. With the tools and knowledge you've acquired, you're well-equipped to make informed decisions that protect your assets, provide for your family, and ensure a lasting impact. As you continue on this path, trust in your ability to navigate the challenges and embrace the opportunities that lie ahead.

Remember, your estate plan is a reflection of your life's work, your values, and your hopes for the future. By taking control of your legacy, you're not only securing your peace of mind but also providing a solid foundation for generations to come. So, go forth with confidence, knowing that you have the power to shape your financial destiny and leave a lasting mark on the world.

SHARE WHAT YOU'VE LEARNED—HELP SOMEONE ELSE PLAN FOR PEACE OF MIND

If you found this book helpful in understanding living trusts, protecting your assets, or feeling more confident about your legacy, would you take a moment to leave a review?

Your feedback could be exactly what another overwhelmed reader needs. So many people put off planning because it feels confusing or intimidating—but your honest review can show them it's possible to move forward with clarity, calm, and purpose.

Whether you learned one new thing or walked away feeling empowered to take the next step, your voice matters.

By sharing your thoughts on Amazon, you're helping to build a community where everyday families—just like yours—can learn how to protect what matters most without fear, legal confusion, or unnecessary expense.

>>> Click the link or scan the QR code below to leave your review on Amazon:

https://www.amazon.com/review/review-your-purchases/?asin=B0F5WW6GFP

Thank you for being part of this movement to demystify estate planning and give others the courage to take action. Let's keep hope—and peace of mind—alive, one family at a time.
With heartfelt gratitude,

Tammi Schneider

GLOSSARY

Beneficiary: A beneficiary is someone who receives assets from a trust or will. Lawsuits may arise over disputes, mismanagement, or denied inheritance.

Bypass trusts: A bypass trust helps reduce estate taxes by passing assets to beneficiaries without exceeding tax exemptions. Disputes may arise over tax issues, mismanagement, or trust terms.

Charitable remainder trusts: A charitable remainder trust lets the grantor donate assets to charity while receiving income during their lifetime. Disputes may arise over tax compliance or mismanagement.

Certificate of trust: A certificate of trust is a document that verifies the existence and terms of a trust without disclosing all the details. Disputes may arise over its validity or the scope of authority granted to the trustee.

Codicil: A codicil is a legal document that modifies, amends, or supplements an existing will without completely rewriting it.

Dynasty trusts: A dynasty trust is designed to provide benefits to multiple generations while minimizing estate taxes. Disputes may arise over trust administration, asset distribution, or tax compliance.

Fiduciary duty: Fiduciary duty is the legal obligation to act in another's best interest. Lawsuits may arise over mismanagement, conflicts of interest, or breach of trust.

Grantor: A grantor is a person who creates a trust or transfers property to another. Legal disputes may arise over capacity, fraud, or coercion in the transfer.

Irrevocable life insurance trust: An irrevocable life insurance trust removes life insurance from the estate for tax purposes. Disputes may arise over trust terms or mismanagement of funds.

Irrevocable trust: An irrevocable trust cannot be changed or revoked once created. Lawsuits may arise over fraud, mismanagement, or disputes about its validity.

Pour-over will: A pour-over will transfer any unallocated assets into a trust upon death. Disputes may arise over validity or asset management.

Probate: Probate is the court process of validating a will and distributing assets. Legal disputes may involve will contests, creditor claims, or executor misconduct.

Revocable trust: A revocable trust is a trust that can be changed or canceled by the grantor during their lifetime. Legal disputes may arise over capacity, undue influence, or improper changes.

Testamentary trust: A testamentary trust is created through a will and takes effect after the person's death. Lawsuits may involve disputes over the will, trust terms, or trustee actions.

Trust agreement: A trust agreement is a legal document outlining the terms and conditions of a trust. Disputes may arise over the interpretation of terms, trustee duties, or beneficiary rights

Trustee: A trustee manages a trust and can face lawsuits for mismanagement or breach of duty.

Special needs trust: A special needs trust is designed to provide for a beneficiary with disabilities without affecting their eligibility for government benefits. Disputes may involve mismanagement, misuse of funds, or failure to meet legal requirements.

REFERENCES

- *What Is a Living Trust?* https://www.investopedia.com/terms/l/living-trust.asp
- *Living Trust vs. Will: What's the Difference? - NerdWallet* https://www.nerdwallet.com/article/investing/estate-planning/living-trust-vs-will#:~:text=A%20last%20will%20and%20testament%20takes%20effect%20upon%20death%20and,the%20benefits%20of%20both%20documents.
- *5 Myths About Trusts You Can't Afford to Believe - LegalZoom* https://www.legalzoom.com/articles/5-myths-about-trusts-you-cant-afford-to-believe#:~:text=Myth%202%3A%20'Living%20trusts%20only,he%20or%20she%20become%20incapacitated.
- *What Is the Average Cost to Prepare a Living Trust?* https://www.legalzoom.com/articles/cost-to-set-up-a-living-trust#:~:text=The%20average%20living%20trust%20

cost,complexity%2C%20location%2C%20and%20approach.

- *How to Create a Living Trust - Protecting Wealth* https://protectingwealth.com/how-to-create-a-living-trust/
- *13 Essential Documents for Every Living Trust-Based* ... https://www.treetownlaw.com/blog/13-essential-documents-for-every-living-trust-based-estate-plan
- *Revocable vs Irrevocable Trust: Differences & Benefits* https://trustandwill.com/learn/revocable-vs-irrevocable-trust?srsltid=AfmBOooYLCttoYn4hSze7Sf8YSCkCMcHAjAHVEQtzPR1whU3RJt-jrWa
- *Seven Common Living Trust Mistakes and How to Avoid Them* https://www.orangecountyestateplanningattorney.com/blog/seven-common-living-trust-mistakes-and-how-to-avoid-them/
- *What are the disadvantages of probate?* https://eblawgroup.com/what-are-the-disadvantages-of-probate/#:~:text=The%20probate%20process%20is%20expensive,a%20hundred%20thousand%20dollar%20estate).
- *How Living Trusts Avoid Probate* https://www.nolo.com/legal-encyclopedia/how-liv

ing-trusts-avoid-probate-29848.html

- *Estate tax | Internal Revenue Service* https://www.irs.gov/businesses/small-businesses-self-employed/estate-tax
- *How to Avoid Estate Taxes With Trusts* https://smartasset.com/estate-planning/how-to-avoid-estate-taxes-with-trusts
- *Two Types of Trusts: Which Protect Against Creditors?* https://www.estateplanning.com/which-type-of-trust-protect-against-creditors
- *Protecting Your Digital Assets through Estate Planning* https://www.evanscase.com/protecting-your-digital-assets-through-estate-planning/
- *Case Study: A Revocable Living Trust for Anonymity &* ... https://houston-probate-law.com/case-study-a-revocable-living-trust-for-anonymity-asset-protection/
- *Blended Families and Estate Planning: What You Should Know?* https://www.eckellsparks.com/2025/02/06/blended-families-estate-planning-2/
- *Choosing the Right Trustee - Fiduciary Trust* https://www.fiduciary-trust.com/insights/choosing-the-right-trustee/
- *fiduciary duties of trustees | Wex - Legal Information In-*

stitute https://www.law.cornell.edu/wex/fiduciary_duties_of_trustees

- *10 Questions to Ask When Interviewing a Corporate ...* https://www.sherwoodfp.com/post/10-questions-to-ask-when-interviewing-a-corporate-trustee-or-professional-fiduciary
- *These Case Studies Hammer Home the Value of a Living ...* https://morristrust.com/these-case-studies-hammer-home-the-value-of-a-living-trust/
- *When Should You Update Your Living Trust and Will* https://www.riluslaw.com/blog/when-should-you-update-your-living-trust-and-will
- *Trusts & Estates 50-State Charts Toolkit | Practical Law* https://content.next.westlaw.com/practical-law/document/Ibe7995a35c0511e79bef99c0ee06c731/Trusts-Estates-50-State-Charts-Toolkit?viewType=FullText&transitionType=Default&contextData=(sc.Default)
- *2023 Estate Planning Industry Trends Survey* https://www.wealthcounsel.com/articles/2023/2023-estate-planning-industry-trends-report
- *Can a Trust Be Changed? Insights for Trustees* https://www.wmtxlaw.com/can-a-trust-be-changed/

- *DIY Living Trust: Should You Do It?* https://www.themckenziefirm.com/diy-living-trust-should-you-do-it

- *What Is the Average Cost to Prepare a Living Trust?* https://www.legalzoom.com/articles/cost-to-set-up-a-living-trust#:~:text=The%20cost%20of%20a%20living,states%20have%20more%20legal%20requirements).

- *How to Prevent and Resolve Conflicts Among Beneficiaries* https://www.bmcestateplanning.com/blog/family-disputes-and-estate-planning

- *Estate Planning for Blended Families: Pitfalls and Solutions* https://www.cunninghamlegal.com/estate-planning-for-blended-families-pitfalls-and-solutions/

- *Estate Planning in Depth: Current Trends 2023* https://www.ali-cle.org/course/Estate-Planning-in-Depth-Current-Trends-2023-CF006

- *Creating A Digital Estate Plan in 4 Steps* https://bluenotary.us/creating-a-digital-estate-plan-4-steps/

- *Leaving a Lasting Legacy: A Scoping Review of Ethical Wills* https://pmc.ncbi.nlm.nih.gov/articles/PMC9636071/#:~:text=They%20provide%20a%20way%20for,have%20been%20utilized%20for%20centuries.

Blockchain in real estate: Recent developments and ...

Checklist

Personal Information

- Full legal names of Grantor(s) and Trustee(s)
- Contact information
- Marital status and spouse's information (if applicable)
- Names and contact info of Successor Trustee(s)
- Names and information for all beneficiaries

Assets to Consider for Inclusion

- Real Estate
- Primary residence
- Vacation homes
- Rental properties
- Undeveloped land
- Timeshares

Other Items to Gather:

- Deeds, mortgage statements, property tax info
- Bank & Financial Accounts
- Checking and savings accounts
- Certificates of Deposit (CDs)
- Money market accounts
- Brokerage/investment accounts:
- Account numbers, institutions, current balances
- Retirement Accounts & Insurance
- IRAs, 401(k)s, pensions (may need special handling — often not retitled)
- Life insurance policies

Gather: Beneficiary designations, policy numbers, plan documents

- Business Interests
- Ownership in LLCs, corporations, or partnerships

Gather: Operating agreements, stock certificates, business valuation

- Valuable Personal Property

- Vehicles, boats, RVs
- Art, jewelry, collectibles
- Firearms

Include receipts or appraisals if available

Other Assets

- Safe deposit boxes
- Intellectual property (patents, copyrights)
- Royalties or mineral rights
- Cryptocurrency wallets or digital assets

Document how to access or transfer these assets

Other Key Documents

- Existing will (if any)
- Durable Power of Attorney
- Health Care Directive/Living Will
- Prenuptial or postnuptial agreements
- Divorce decrees or child support agreements
- Titles, deeds, or legal ownership papers

Instructions & Special Requests

- Guardianship nominations (if minors are involved)

- Specific bequests (gifts of items or amounts)
- Charitable contributions
- Wishes for handling digital assets or social media accounts

www.ingramcontent.com/pod-product-compliance
Lightning Source LLC
LaVergne TN
LVHW050915210926
848482LV00012B/453